WOMEN LIKE ME

RECLAIMING OUR POWER

JULIE FAIRHURST

ROCK STAR PUBLISHING

COMPILED BY JULIE FAIRHURST
Julie Fairhurst – Rock Star Publishing
Paperback Edition: ISBN 978-1-990639-12-8
Cover Design and Interior Design by STOKE Publishing

The authors of this book do not dispense medical advice or prescribe the use of any technique as a form of treatment for physical, emotional, or medical problems without a physician's advice, either directly or indirectly. The authors intend to provide general information to individuals taking positive steps in their lives for emotional and spiritual well-being. If you use any information in this book for yourself, which is your constitutional right, the authors and the publishers assume no responsibility for your actions.

At times, some readers may be triggered by a women's story. Should you need to speak with someone, there are many crisis lines, counselors, and doctors that you can reach out to. Find someone that can lend a kind ear to listen to you. That can be a friend, parent, spouse, or anyone you trust. Your local community services may have telephone numbers to assist you.

CONTENTS

"It took me quite a long time to develop a voice, and now that
I have it, I am not going to be silent."

Madeleine Albright

INTRODUCTION

Women Like Me: Reclaiming Our Power is a powerful and inspiring book that celebrates the strength and resilience of women who, against all odds, have overcome the challenges in their lives and claimed their power.

This book is a collection of personal stories from a diverse group of women who come from different cultural and socioeconomic backgrounds.

Despite their differences, these women all share one thing in common: they have faced adversity and oppression, and they have fought back. It is a collection of stories by incredible women who have faced adversity and overcome it. It is an inspiring reminder that no matter what life throws our way, we have the power to rise above it and reclaim our power. Each story is different, but they all share a common thread: the power of perseverance.

This book is a collection of stories by incredible women who have faced adversity and overcome it. It is an inspiring reminder that no matter what life throws our way, we have the power to rise above it and reclaim our power. Each story is different, but they all share a common thread: the power of perseverance.

In these pages, you will find stories of strength, courage, and hope. These women are proof that no challenge is too great, and that no obstacle is insurmountable. They are a testament to the power of the human spirit, and their ability to persevere in the face of adversity is truly inspiring.

The women who contributed to this book are not only sharing their stories of survival, but they are also helping others to heal by sharing their own journeys. By sharing their experiences, these women are inspiring others to find their own voices and share their stories.

They are helping to create a culture of healing and empowerment, and they are doing their part to end the cycle of violence. By sharing our stories, we can help each other heal. We can find strength in each other's words, and we can find hope in each other's actions. We can create a culture of healing and empowerment, and we can end the cycle of violence.

By sharing our stories, we can change the world. The women who have written in this book are not only telling their own stories; they are also giving other women permission to tell their stories. They are showing that survivors are not alone and that they are not defined by their abuse. They are showing the world that survivors are strong and that they can find their own power.

Julie Fairhurst

Founder of Women Like Me

"I raise up my voice—not so that I can shout, but so that those without a voice can be heard. … We cannot all succeed when half of us are held back."

Malala Yousafzai

PART 1

RECLAIMING OUR POWER

"Always remember that you are absolutely unique.
Just like everyone else."

Margaret Mead

WHO'S THAT BEAUTIFUL WOMAN IN THE MIRROR?

Finally, Finding My Way To A Life Of Body, Kindness, and Love After 40 Years

"Your worry doesn't change outcomes; Your presence does."
Anne Caissie

Sixteen years old. That's how old I was when I remember being wildly aware of the size of my hips, the curve of my stomach, the width of my thighs, and how my butt looked in jeans. I distinctly recall thinking they were ALL WRONG.

I was a 5'8", 99 pounds, with a 22" waist, perfect teeth teenage girl whose collar bones could be seen from clear across the room. And I truly and honestly believed I was fat.

Fast forward several years. I did what many of us do. I had children, got married, and started living a "regular life." I was busy! Non-stop days of two full-time jobs, one outside of the house and the other inside the house. My typical day started at 5 or 6 a.m. with at least half a pot of strong black coffee. Then lunches had to get packed because even though I'd planned on packing them the night before, this task just never seemed to get done. Then the battle began to get the kids up, fed, dressed, and out the door to school. In between all this activity, I somehow managed to brush my teeth, comb my hair, and put on some clothes that passed the sniff test, and after getting the kids to their destination, I was off to work.

I would arrive at work and would proceed to subsist on more coffee all morning. Lunch would roll around, and I'd grab whatever fast-food meal was closest to my office or not. There were, in fact, more days than not that I'd go without lunch, telling myself that I really shouldn't spend the money on just myself. By the time the end of the work day rolled around, I would be so hungry that I'd stop at the drive-thru on the way home and "snack" on not one but two burgers.

Arriving home, I'd be in a rush to prepare a dinner of some sort. I never had a plan, so I ended up throwing something frozen in the oven and opening up a can of veggies. This had to be done quickly because most nights, there was an activity that one of the kids needed a ride to. Baseball games, Girl Guides, soccer practices, etc., took up at least three of the five weekday evenings. While the kids ate, I'd be scouring the house for various pieces of equipment for the game or the Girl Guide sash that was required for the uniform. And then, swoosh, we'd be out the door again.

By 7 or 8 p.m., we'd all be back at home. I'd be hollering up the stairs to the kids to remind them to brush their teeth and get their pj's on. Tucking them into bed, I'd think, 'I should pack the lunches for tomorrow.' But then I'd make my way back downstairs and think about how tired I was and pour myself a big glass of wine because, darn it, I worked hard today! I deserved it!

My schedule got more challenging as time passed. In fact, it got busier and busier as the kids grew and found more interests. My husband worked long hours and traveled extensively for work, so when he was home, he wasn't truly engaged or interested in doing anything but relaxing at home.

The glass of wine turned into a bottle of wine over the years. I stopped worrying about my appearance. I stopped any form of self-care. Come on! I was busy! The slippery slope was right in front of me, and I jumped right on. Binge eating, too much alcohol, no exercise of any kind, and a general sense of apathy.

And then my 25-year relationship ended, seemingly just like that, when my husband packed a bag and walked out the door to a new relationship. I spent the next year mired in grief and self-blame, and self-hatred. I somehow made myself believe that how I looked was why my marriage had failed. I started telling myself that if I hadn't gained so much weight or had taken the time to put on makeup in the mornings, my marriage would surely have worked out. I took on all the blame. And that blame caused more of the same destructive behavior.

For the next year, I survived on pre-packaged or fast food. I gained more weight. I drank at least a bottle of wine a night. I barely made it through my workday, doing just enough not to draw too much attention to the fact that I just didn't care about my job.

I sat in front of the television on my couch from the end of the work day until I woke up uncomfortable and bleary-eyed, having passed out at some point in the evening. I'd shuffle off to bed only to lay there wide awake and berate myself for my behavior. I'd wonder if I'd lose 50 pounds if everything would be better because I'd look better and feel better, and I could meet someone new, and life would be perfect!

And then, one day, I just stopped.

I told myself that I could not go on the way I was. My daughters were worried; my friends were dropping hints that they were concerned. My boss was starting to complain about my job performance. I had to do something. I had to give my whole system a jolt. I had to make a significant, bold change.

So, 1 hopped on a plane to Cuba. I had to get away from everything and everyone. I couldn't really afford the trip, but I knew if I wanted to survive, I had to do something.

I spent most of that week in Cuba, walking the beach. I don't know to this day how many miles I walked, but let's just say it was a lot! I lay in the sun. I ate real food. I slept. I sat on the beach a watched the water. I cried. I cried a lot.

But at some point, close to the end of that week in Cuba, I felt it. That little glimmer of hope and power. It started deep, deep down in my body. I felt it rising up, up to my chest and my heart. It got stuck for a while in my throat but then BOOM! There it was! Me! I was ready! I was ready to forgive myself for it all. For allowing myself to come last. For allowing myself to feel like I didn't matter. For allowing myself to think that my physical shape dictated who I was and for allowing myself to be invisible.

I returned from Cuba knowing that I was ready to take responsibility for how my life was going to unfold going forward. I was ready to do the work. I promised myself that I wouldn't give up when it got hard. And believe me; it did get hard.

What I decided to do was basically Marie Kondo my entire life. Marie Kondo is a decluttering and organization phenom! She asks you to really focus on what to keep in your home (or, in my case, my life!) by examining each item and deciding if it "sparks joy." If it does, it stays; If it doesn't, you release it with gratitude! I started with my nutrition and moved into my exercise. From there, I tackled all other areas of my life. The more joy I brought into my life, the happier I became. I started to feel better physically, then emotionally.

I started caring about my appearance again and found such happiness in simple, everyday tasks. Washing my face with warm water became such an immense delight. Preparing a fresh salad in my own kitchen and sitting at the table to eat felt like a special occasion. Heading out for a walk all bundled up in a warm sweater felt like I was experiencing my town for the first time. Experiencing the feeling of the delight of having the sun's warmth on my face.

Being present in my life allowed me to transform my mind, body, and soul. This is where I think we all sometimes get stuck. We forget that we have to look at all of ourselves and not just the pounds we've gained or the dreams we've put on the back burner. We also allow ourselves to get into that "all or nothing" mindset where we think there's no sense even bothering since there's no way we can do it all right now. But if we start with one simple step, we can succeed! I picked something incredibly simple; I made myself a salad for dinner.

That is not to say that it was easy. Nor was it all joy and bliss every step of the way. Believe me! That is not the case at all. I had many missteps. I often and easily slipped back into old patterns and behaviors. But this is where the promise I made to myself on that beach in Cuba came in. Yes, I promised myself that I would change. That I would do the hard work. But I also promised that I would give myself grace.

I often reminded myself of a quote one of my first Yoga teachers shared. Dianne Bondy explained that "grace happens to give us some space, acceptance, and room to take a hard swallow or step back. Grace isn't an excuse for feeling less inner or interpersonal conflict but an opportunity to be kind to yourself".

Over the last number of years, I have transformed my attitude toward my body image. I've reset the way that I look at dieting and exercise. And I've reached many of the goals I've set for myself.

And today I'm happy. Just the way I am.

ANNE CAISSIE

"I am a woman with thoughts and questions and shit to say. I say if I'm beautiful. I say if I'm strong. You will not determine my story—I will."

Amy Schumer

2

FROM CITY SLICKER
TO COUNTRY PICKER

"And suddenly you just know...it's time to start something new
and trust the magic of new beginnings."
Meister Eckhart

It's early morning as I sit on the deck watching the sunrise through the Poplars. The air is just slightly chilled, and the steam rises from my coffee. As the sun peaks over the trees and the sky fills with cotton candy clouds, I begin to feel the warmth on my skin and a gentle breeze.

My view is breathtaking, with its lush green valley spreading out before me and the majestic mountains rising up behind it, trying to reach the pink and orange clouds above. The sunlight plays across the mountains and the valley below, casting long shadows and creating a mesmerizing scene before me. I can hear the sounds of nature all around, from the rustling of leaves in the trees to the chirping of the birds waking from their slumber. The air is so fresh and clean, and I feel a sense of peace and tranquility wash over me. I feel so rejuvenated and inspired.

2021

Well, the cleaning is all done and ready for the new owners. As I stand in the entrance of the empty townhouse, my heart and mind filled with memories of our last ten years here, the rooms, once filled with laughter and love, now echo with emptiness, the warmth of our things all gone.

As I turn for one last time and close the door, my eyes well up with tears that threaten to pour. I walk down the driveway towards my car, and there, my good friend stands waiting with open arms.

We embrace tightly, trying to hold back the emotions we feel, so hard to explain. Goodbyes are never easy. They cut like a knife, leaving behind a piece of ourselves and our life. I tell her we will see each other soon, "I love you."

As I drive away and look in my rear-view mirror, I see her standing there, waving goodbye, with a heart full of care. The tears blur my vision as I leave behind a life we once knew.

Highway bound, my mind races with thoughts of the past, present, and future, all tied in knots. Excitement and sadness are mixed up in a brew as we embark on this journey to a new place.

Leaving behind family and friends is heart-wrenching, but we know that in life, change is a must. As we travel down this uncertain road, we hold onto hope, and a new life will unfold.

As we drove past Hope in beautiful British Columbia, the sun started to set behind the mountains, casting a warm glow across the sky. The canyon highway was the choice we made that would take us to Chasm, where our 5th wheel sat parked on the doorstep of our generous in-laws' home. It was a symbol of their unwavering support and love during our search for a new property. The emotions within me were mixed, gratefulness, apprehension, and anxiety all swirling within me.

The year 2021 had been plagued with fires, and as we approached Lytton, it was almost dark. The destruction and devastation we witnessed left me speechless, and the once-beautiful mountainous scenery now looked like the apocalypse lit up in the sky like a massive fireball. I was consumed with fear and overwhelmed by what I saw.

We turned a bend on the highway, and the skies were lit up with flames and smoke engulfing the mountainsides. The smoke made it difficult to see, and the fire was burning right beside the road, and the entire mountains on both sides were engulfed in flames. We had driven into hell. I watched my husband disappear in the billowing clouds of smoke, and panic set in. He was driving in front of me and had now vanished. I slowed to a crawl, and the dogs and I clung to each other, praying to make it through the inferno unscathed.

It felt like an eternity before we made it out of the blaze, but it was just a few moments before my husband's truck appeared in front of me again, and as I looked in my rear-view mirror, they were shutting down the Highway behind me. The thoughts of what we had done and the fear of what might have happened to us raced through my mind. But we had made it through, and that was all that mattered.

As we continued our journey, I couldn't help but wonder what other obstacles lay ahead. The road ahead was uncertain and frightening, but we had each other, and that was enough to give us the courage to move forward.

After about six weeks of searching for the perfect home, we were starting to feel like Goldilocks. Nothing was just right, or it was too small or too big or just too damn weird. We saw homes that were way too close to the highways. I was afraid we'd have to start a new business cleaning up roadkill!! But then, my husband suggested we take a look at a property that was a bit further out from town. I thought, "Are you NUTS"; I didn't want to live in the middle of nowhere. But he insisted it would be a nice drive even if we did not like it, and I reluctantly agreed to go.

Let me tell you, it was a LONG drive. I was starting to wonder if we had accidentally driven all the way to Narnia. I thought we were lost in the wilderness! But then, we turned a corner, and BOOM! This breathtaking view of the valley and mountains just appeared before our eyes. I swear our mouths were hanging open like two cartoon characters.

We were so blown away. We immediately called the real estate agent, who thankfully lived just 15 minutes away.

The property was a 23-acre hobby farm with more acreage than we were looking for. However, complete with a house, barns, paddocks, a hay field, and a view to die for.

But let me tell you, the inside of the house was defiantly not what we were looking for. It had good bones but was a fixer-upper, to say the least. We immediately saw the potential and put in an offer the very next day.

Then the real fun began. The struggle with the current owner was no joke. Let's just say they were not thrilled to be selling. It was like negotiating with a grumpy toddler. But in the end, we came out victorious and signed on the dotted line.

Now the real adventure begins, fixing up the inside of the house. Time to break out the tool belts and hard hats! Let's just hope we don't get lost on our way home from the grocery store!

Well, hot diggity dang (that's farmers' lingo if you are wondering, laughing), we got ourselves a couple of almost farmers over here! Can you imagine owning a farm? It sounds like a blast, right? We were so pumped that we even decided to get ourselves some new farm animals right away to occupy our barns – Mila and Miguel, our goats. Now let me tell you, life was perfect until after a month when my husband had to return to work.

He was traveling back and forth from the west coast until October when he officially retired, and I was stuck in the middle of Butt Nutt nowhere, all by myself! I mean, who leaves their wife alone in the middle of nowhere with goats and dogs, and they are not great conversationalists, I can tell ya that!

And then it happened! One night when the dogs were barking like they saw a ghost, it was 1:00 am in the morning. I jumped out of bed, and the dogs were already at the front door, ready to pounce. So, I did what any sane person would do. I grabbed the gun in the corner and opened the door, aiming into the darkness.

But here's the thing, I was butt naked, and it was just a wee bit chilly outside. I mean, I looked like Annie Oakley on a bender, and let's just say it was not my best look. I stepped out onto the front deck, ready to take on the world, and realized there was nothing there. It was just me, a gun with no magazine or bullets (that's right, I forgot to load the gun). I am sure there was a deer out there staring at me like I was a nut job. I came back into the house feeling like a complete fool and laughing at myself. Needless to say, I didn't get any more sleep that night, but hey, at least I had a good story to tell! And a most important lesson, not to forget to check your damn gun before you go out to shoot the big monsters at 1:00 am in the morning!

The struggle was real for me, y'all. The transition going from the city to the farm was like going from a fancy steak dinner to eating grass (not that I would know what that's like). I mean, where was the mall I could walk to? The convenience store on the corner? The ability to call up a friend or one of my kids for a quick lunch or breakfast or ask my sisters over for dinner. It was like I was living in the Stone Age!

And don't even get me started on the food. No more Pad Thai, butter chicken, or Chinese food delivered to my doorstep. At least I learned how to make my own takeout, which really means frozen lasagna and garlic bread. Talk about gourmet, baby! I thought I was gonna die!

And then there was the lack of sirens, rush hour traffic, and the grossness of the pollution. WHERE WAS ALL THE NOISE? How am I supposed to know what time it is without a car horn blaring every five seconds (laughing)?

But seriously, as time went on, I started to appreciate the beauty of the countryside. With the fresh air, the lack of sirens, and rush hour traffic and pollution, our rush hour traffic now consists of the deer and moose crossing our road or the squirrels running around hiding their nuts. I now enjoy the peaceful sounds of nature. Sure, the nearest town is a 30-minute drive, but we learned to adjust. And when we want to splurge, we hit up the Chinese restaurant in town or the pub for my favorite beef dip, even if it means driving on the highway at night (cue the fear of hitting a deer or moose). But hey, we made it work and eventually learned to appreciate the simple life.

Oh my gosh, who needs a fancy-pants university degree when you have YouTube and a bunch of barnyard animals? My husband and I are like the MacGyvers of the farm world. Last year, we had our first lambing, and we were so clueless when it came to lambing, but let me tell you, it was like a scene from an action movie. We watched more lambing videos on YouTube than I've watched dog videos on Instagram (and that's saying something). But somehow, we managed to pull it off, and now we're like the sheep midwives of the Cariboo (laughing).

This year, we're taking it up a notch and lambing hopefully 20 little fluff balls in March. I'm both excited and terrified at the same time, but lambing is amazing, and being there to see those beauties coming into the world, it's the most exhilarating feeling.

And let's not forget about our stinky pigs. We get piglets at the end of March and then leave the farm by October first. I leave the pig wrangling to my husband because let's be real, they stink worse than a frat house on Sunday morning (laughing). But it's all worth it because we have a freezer full of fresh meat (note: I leave the farm when it's time to butcher.)

We even have our own army of egg-laying chickens producing more eggs than the Easter Bunny. We also added a new addition to the farm family this year, and our two Great Pyrenees had a puppy. Yes, just one puppy, thank gawd! We tried our best to keep them apart, but they had a fly-by behind the barn (laughing). This brings us to the whomping number of six dogs (laughing). We rescued two of our dogs last year, one is deaf, and one was abused.

We used to have goats too, but last year we had to make a tough decision between goats and sheep. We were not able to increase both as we did not have room. We chose sheep because, let's face it, they're way cuter, fluffier, and easier to manage. We even named all our breeding sheep after herbs, like Thyme and Mint and other herbs (don't judge us laughing).

Our greenhouse is going to be the envy of all the neighbors this year (I hope, with a little help from my friends). We're going to grow so many veggies that we'll be able to stock up on everything for winter. Ugh, I see lots of canning and freeze-drying in my future. Our goal is to be "farmed to table" by the end of the year, which basically means we'll be self-sufficient and won't need to depend on the grocery store rip-offs as much.

Living in the Cariboo has been an eye-opening experience for us. We've learned so much about taking care of ourselves in a healthier way (although we still indulge in the occasional burger when we can).

We have an open-door policy on the farm as we have lots of space for everyone, which means friends and family can come here anytime to help on the farm or just enjoy nature and visit. It's like a revolving party door, except instead of beer and pizza, we have manure and hay (laughing). We have made many friends in the time we have been here who share the same passion for farm life. And the best part? We never have to go to the grocery store for meat again. Take that, Save On Food!

I want to tell all you lovely readers out there that it's never too late to pursue your dreams. My husband and I retired back in 2021, and although some may argue that running a farm is work, we believe it's more about reaping the rewards of your efforts and cherishing the beauty and abundance it offers.

We have always loved the four seasons and enjoy the beauty of each one as they pass through our little piece of paradise. Don't be afraid to step out of your comfort zone, forget about looking before you leap, and just go for it! If one path doesn't work out, there are always more adventures waiting for you around the corner.

In my opinion, farm life is the best kind of lifestyle - it's unique and enriching. Oh, and one last thing I forgot to mention was the hot cowboys (laughing).

Well, I gotta go collect some eggs now (grinning ear to ear).

Whispering Winds Farm in Cariboo, BC. Signing off!

BRENDA COOPER

"Justice is about making sure that being polite is not the same thing as being quiet. In fact, often times, the most righteous thing you can do is shake the table."

Alexandria Ocasio-Cortez

3

FINDING GRATEFULNESS IN GRIEF

The Journey of a Deep-seeded Friendship Through Love and Loss Transformed into Daily Gratitude

"Those we love… don't go away. They walk beside us every day. Unseen, unheard, but always near, still loved still missed, and forever dear." Unknown

For over three months, I had been texting my girlfriend daily, sending her messages, gifs, and images. Until I stopped receiving her replies. The last text was a gif I sent of a person holding over a dozen roses with the message "special delivery for you." Her reply followed with a message; "Thanks, love you." It was at that moment I knew; things had changed.

My girlfriend, Janine, was like a sister to me. We had been friends for over 20 years. I also was blessed to have her stand up with me on my wedding day as one of my two maids of honor.

There was no way I could decide between these two incredibly special ladies in my life.

Janine, Amanda, and I all met in our twenties. Amanda and I became friends first as we met through working at an after-school program called Mad Science. We talked outside of work one day for hours beside our cars. We have been friends ever since that day. Amanda introduced me to Janine during one of her house parties. Janine and I talked and laughed at that party.

The three of us would hang out, go for coffee, and go shopping, which by the way, was one of Janine's favorite activities to do. In her closet, you would find clothes that still had the tags on them. We always told her she should be a fashion designer. Janine loved fashion and always found the cutest outfits or accessories for herself and others. She had a natural eye for it.

One of our favorite girlfriend traditions was to get together in Fort Langley, go for coffee at Blacksmith Bakery, and explore the cute little vintage shops. We looked forward to our meeting as we discussed how we would all be old ladies one day sitting here laughing and reminiscing about our younger days. We laughed about how we would have to buy cute little old lady hats to cover our gray hair.

I remember the first time we visited our favorite spot without our girl. Amanda had arrived before me and got us a table. At first, I didn't notice, but Amanda had placed three chairs around the table. She told me this one was for Janine. My heart was aching, but Amanda didn't have to say anything. We knew she was there in our hearts. Fort Langley is home to a variety of local shops, galleries, breweries, and eateries that have been featured in many movies and TV shows. We loved visiting our favorite shop on the corner every time Janine came into town, and now we still go to

Fort Langley in her honor and have a cup of coffee together, only now, we share different stories with Janine in our hearts.

Years after we met, Janine and I were roommates before we eventually married our husbands. Janine knew I loved coffee and would always have a coffee ready for me in the morning. We enjoyed many nights in our pajamas chatting, laughing, and watching some favorite shows together, such as Sex in the City and Amazing Race. We helped each other through many of life's defining moments where one of us had a major life change. Together we went through some individual defining moments, from getting married, getting divorced, starting a new job or leaving an old one, taking a big trip, finishing school, and having a baby, to name a few.

Janine and I, years ago, traveled together to Europe. We went to visit her parents in Scotland. This trip was very important to both of us, but it almost didn't happen. I had recently lost my job and didn't quite have enough money saved to go. It was May of 2006, during the days when I was a working University student. I was heartbroken and didn't want to tell Janine I couldn't go with her. However, my parents knew how much I enjoyed traveling and paid for the amount I hadn't saved so that I could enjoy the experience with Janine. My mom and dad have always been so supportive of me, and I am grateful to them.

Traveling with Janine was a lifetime experience that cannot be replaced, and I am so grateful that money didn't change that experience. During one of our last conversations, we laughed and relived many moments we shared on that trip. We saw four countries together: Scotland, England, Ireland, and Portugal. I am so glad I made a scrapbook of our trip and wrote down all our highlights.

Back in early April of 2021, Janine mentioned to me she was having some health issues. Little did I know how serious it was and how quickly it would progress. Within a few weeks of numerous doctor visits and emergency room trips, she was told she had cancer. Now, cancer is so scary for anyone because we now enter the unknown and have to shift our faith and thoughts. So many different emotions begin to flow into our souls. But no one could prepare me for the journey ahead.

Then came the phone call that shook my world. I could not believe the words she had just said. It was a glorious sunny day, but my heart was breaking inside for Janine. She told me she only had a few months to live. I remember her saying "that it is a hard pill to swallow." How could you not agree with her words? The only words I could say while sobbing in tears were, "I am so sorry, no! " However, we still had hope at this point. So, many emotions swirled around inside me, and questions flooded my thoughts.

After that conversation, my worries and anxiety increased, but this wasn't the only stressor I was dealing with at that moment. I was teaching at a school I loved, which was being redesigned, as the new school was about to open the following year. The area where I worked had a huge growing population due to recent developments, and the school could no longer keep up with the demands of the growing infrastructure.

Our staff was being divided, as some of us chose to post out to the new school and others decided to stay. I was lucky enough to be given the opportunity to work at the brand-new school in the fall. But that meant I had to pack up my classroom.

Meanwhile, we also made the decision to move into another community. Three of life's most significant stressors all at the same time while still dealing with Covid 19 restrictions as well. Looking back, I wondered how I managed—honestly, love and support from my community of family and friends. At the time, I don't even think I realized how stressed out I was. I just kept going every day.

I remember during one of our many phone conversations. I asked Janine if I could contact her husband and see how he was doing. I wanted to check in and make sure he was being supported. After Janine gave me Michael's number, I called him right away. He answered, and we engaged in a conversation that led us both to tears. I still can't even imagine how he must have been feeling, and the last thing I wanted was for him to feel alone or not supported. I am so glad; we talked that day on the phone. He made me realize the importance of reaching out and listening to each other. He told me how hard it was to go home to his house as they had recently moved in. Janine decorated the house and made it lovely. He said, "It was so hard to go home to my beautifully decorated home done by my wife."

During this time, she was in and out of the hospitals. I know our conversation didn't change the outcome, but at that moment, I knew someone else understood the pain of loving someone so much. I believe it is important to not only check in with the person suffering but everyone around them as well. Everyone needs support during these challenging moments in life. I want to encourage everyone to check in with anyone who surrounds a person suffering.

Another strange struggle I faced during this time was pondering visiting her while restrictions were being put in place for Covid-19. We were still in the midst of a global pandemic. The entire world felt bizarre to me at this moment in time. I lived in the

Lower Mainland, and she lived about three hours away in the Thompson Okanagan Region of Beautiful British Columbia, yet it was being cut off with restrictions. Our government used the power of the Emergency Program Act to prohibit non-essential travel between the three regional zones within the province.

Where I lived, Lower Mainland and Fraser Valley were one. She lived in the Northern/Interior Health zone. Essential travel only, everyone was being advised to stay within their local community. It was strange enough not to be able to travel out of our country but within, too. It just wasn't making any sense to me. So many questions flooded my mind, how could I not be allowed to visit my friend? Should I go? Was it right to go? Did everyone involved have their vaccinations? So many questions and so many unknowns.

All of this left me with a tornado of emotions inside. I felt heartbroken, angry, sad, lost, confused, love, hopeful, and overwhelmed. I was lost in my own emotions. In the end, I made the heartbreaking decision not to go. They say everything happens for a reason, and it wasn't the last time I saw her. When restrictions were lifted, I went with my family up for a visit, and that's when I began to open my eyes to a world of gratitude, she left me with.

During this visit, she opened my eyes to what was truly important in life. We were sitting at her kitchen table, enjoying a cup of tea, and having a conversation. When in the middle, she stopped and turned to me and said, "get your camera and take a picture that is so cute." Here she had noticed how my two boys were chatting and sitting at the top of the stairway, engaged in their own conversation. So, I did take that picture, and it serves as a reminder to me to stop and be present in the current moment and recognize how lucky and blessed I am to be here. I love that picture because it freezes me at that moment in time. A moment I will cherish forever in my life. My boys continue to grow, and I continue to be grateful for my friends and family every day.

After the visit to her home, I did see her one last night. The last time I saw her, she had trouble speaking and struggling to complete her thoughts. I remember holding her hand, hugging her, and telling her how much I loved her. She kept trying to say something to me, but she couldn't get the words out. Her mom and my other best friend Amanda were trying to help. They kept telling me she was trying to say thank you for the flowers because that is who she was. A person who expressed gratitude and always said thank you.

Then, it finally happened. The cancer spread, and nothing more could be done. She passed away in palliative care with her loving husband at her side.

After her passing, I kept finding feathers in my daily life. It all started with a text from my husband when he found one. It explained that feathers were seen as a symbol of acknowledgment that someone or something in the spirit world is looking out for you, keeping you safe, and empowering you to whatever path you set to travel. If you find a feather, your angel is said to be near you, and they are reminding you that you are safe.

After that text, I would find feathers in strange places I could not explain. I found feathers everywhere. My son would even bring me feathers and say, "Look, mom, it is for you from your friend Janine." I started collecting them and keeping them in a container. I found feathers inside my house multiple times on my runs or inside my vehicle or home. I couldn't explain where they were all coming from except I knew they were messages from her and that I would be ok.

I remember one day, I was playing in my youngest son's room with Playmobil, and I looked down and saw a tiny white feather on my leg. Another strange feather experience happened at work during our Terry Fox Run. I signed up that year to be part of the committee to help organize this event at our school. While during the run, a random student ran past me and said, "Look, look, look" he was holding a blue feather in his hand. At that moment, I didn't know what to think. We had over 520 students running outside around the school, and the strange part, I had no idea who that student was. He just kept running after he showed me the feather. I had a few tears roll down my face, and I kept running for the cure. To this day, I have no idea how it got there. There were other moments like this as well.

My husband made all these beautiful moments into a glorious bird painting from the feathers I found, and it hangs as a reminder in our kitchen today.

At first, the grief overtook me, and I remember sobbing on the phone with my dad and saying, "I just want my friend back." At that moment, he just listened and validated my feelings.

It wasn't until after her passing that I reflected on that visit and decided to make a change in my life and be grateful and express gratitude daily. While grieving, I decided to change my life by practicing daily gratitude. I wanted to carry what she was trying so hard to tell me the last time I saw her. Gratitude changed my life. Now I will continue to be grateful for this life and remember to say the two words she often said, Thank you.

To this day, I continue to practice and teach gratitude to others. Every night, I write in a journal three things I am grateful for. I also have taught my students about gratitude and created community gratitude challenges, and sent numerous letters of gratitude and appreciation to others. The responses I received have been incredible and have helped me stay focused on making this world a better place, one step at a time.

My friend Janine taught me to be thankful. Even in her physically weakest moments, she always chose to show gratitude. I will continue to choose gratitude as well.

TRACY DIONNE

"It's important to teach our female youth that it's OK to say, 'Yes,
I am good at this,' and you don't hold back."

Simone Biles

4

LITTLE GIRL LOOKING TO BE LOVED
FINDING THE LOVE THAT CHANGED HER LIFE

"We do not believe in ourselves until someone reveals that deep inside us something is valuable, worth listening to, worthy of our trust, sacred to our touch. Once we believe in ourselves, we can risk curiosity, wonder, spontaneous delight, or any experience that reveals the human spirit." E. E. Cummings

A blizzard was raging. The newscaster said it was "one of the most severe blizzards in Michigan history. It lasted two days, so we were off from school. It was heavy snowfall and very windy. The wet snow on the bottom layers was heavy to lift, and it kept sticking to the shovel. Dad made us help shovel the driveway so he could get out. Our driveway was two cars wide, and it was long.

It was frigid outside; the snow was blowing, and I was freezing. I was tired, my back was hurting, and it was hard to breathe. I asked my dad if I could go into the house and be done shoveling. He laughed at me because I was crying and said, "What's the matter with you?" And then he laughed at me for being a "baby and told me to keep shoveling." He needed help.

It hurt and angered me to feel that my dad didn't care about me. I was only 11 or 12 years old, and I didn't usually act like this, but I was hurting, and he didn't even ask me about how I was. He finally let me go in when I finished the section I was working on.

I was close to the same age when I told my parents, "I need to talk with both of you." We had a meeting then. I usually was not that forward and rarely expressed my feelings, but this day I went right up to them and just blurted it out. My dad asked me, "What is this about?" I told them, "I don't feel like you love me." My dad said to my mom, "Did you hear that, Nora? She doesn't feel like we love her." Mom did not say anything, and my dad laughed. I said, "You never tell me you love me." I started to cry after that because it made me feel like my dad was making fun of me and he didn't think my feelings were legitimate. I felt sad and empty inside. I was afraid of my dad's response; he often embarrassed me when I asked for things. I just wanted to know that they did love me. My mother said they did love me. I think my mom was sad that I felt that way, and she looked hurt.

The feeling of not being loved by my father stretches back further than this. My mother told me that once, I was a baby, and I was crying during the night, so she was rocking me. My father came and took me so Mom could return to bed. When I would not fall asleep, my father just put me on the floor crying and went back to bed. Soon my mother heard me and was up looking for me. After hearing that, it made me wonder if he ever loved me and if he knew how to show love.

When my sister came along, she became the one that was "cute and funny" and knew just how to get out of trouble and avoid spankings. Whenever I heard them talking, I felt ugly, put down, and unimportant, and I was never referred to as cute or funny. We were nothing like each other as we grew up.

In my early school years, I was quiet in class. It was not easy to participate in group activities like reading because we had to read aloud. Some of the time, I was slower than other students in learning because of shyness. I had these feelings even though I got good grades. I do not remember my parents reading to us or having us read to them, and conversations were always very short.

In our family, there wasn't much interaction. Everyone just did their own thing. We did things as a family but not often because of Dad's work schedule. That made me wonder how everybody else lived in their families.

I read books at every opportunity I had. For example, I stayed in my room and read, took books in the car, and went outside in the yard. The books were about families with children. When I was reading, I put myself in the book and lived in a fantasy world where I was part of that family, living like they lived, being loved, and fused over. I was always looking for an opportunity to be a special part of someone's life who would treat me like I was special, cute, and worthy of being loved.

I didn't realize at the time how much or why I was doing this, but now, after doing deep inner work on myself, I do. I didn't attach the behavior to not feeling loved. I just felt good when I was reading and putting myself in the story. I wanted to be liked but didn't think I deserved it. I had a bad feeling about myself, and my thoughts and self-talk were negative. It seemed like I was always doing things wrong or wasn't doing enough to help around the house.

I don't remember getting hugs, kisses, being told I was cute, pretty, cuddled, or any of those endearing behaviors. In fact, one time, I went to give my dad a goodbye kiss as he left for work, and he said, "I don't want a kiss from you."

As part of our family, I always enjoyed going to church. I went to church with my friend as often as I could because the people included me, they were nice to me, and every time I went, they remembered me. I felt like I belonged.

At that church, I came to know Jesus and asked him into my heart. That was very special, all the people came to me and congratulated me and hugged me. I never thought about it at the time. It was just a feeling of jealousy when I saw other kids interacting with their parents. I felt jealous because I wanted to be held close, cuddled, and told, "I love you." I just stuffed all these feelings deep into my memory.

Despite not believing I was as smart as people thought, I tried to please my parents and others to be accepted and worthy of their love. I spent much of my free time studying and reading to ensure I was doing my best. It never seemed to work because people came in and out of my life, and I always felt like I was left behind, didn't fit in, and didn't quite make the grade.

As time passed, I worked hard to be better so people would like me and be my friend. I tried to make changes in myself and figure out what I was doing wrong. But I could not figure it out. I hid my feelings about being unable to make friends that stuck around. I didn't want them to find out it made me angry or that it hurt. People always told me I take things too personally. One friend once told me I was very "sarcastic." So, I tried changing that, and I have been able to reduce the sarcasm. Sometimes it gets in my way.

When my dad was home from work he did not play with us most days. I played outside with kids on the block or by myself. Dad worked long hours. He was tired, and if he didn't have chores, he usually fell asleep on the couch watching TV. Sometimes he took us on picnics with friends or by ourselves. I never noticed my dad smile or laugh often. Sometimes we got to go to the Ice Capades, which I loved. It was always exciting because Mom used to watch the 'ice skating' competitions on TV every year with me. In those days, going for a car ride on Sunday afternoons was the big outing, but it only allowed a little interaction. I took books to read. Sometimes we stopped for ice cream cones.

One of my favorite activities was playing was 'house.' My next favorite activity was playing school with my animals and dolls and chalkboard. I knew I wanted to be a nurse or teacher. I played house and school; I entered my fantasy about life the way I wanted it to be. I wanted to be a wife and a mom most of all.

I cherish the 'special' things I did when growing up, going to Girl Scout camp, going to Guelph, where all my family and I were born, every summer for a few weeks, and staying with aunts and uncles. I felt like one of their family. I felt loved. I cried when I had to go home, and one time after I got home, I turned around and went back. My neighbor drove me halfway back, and my grandparents came halfway to meet us. Everybody thought I was being silly, and they did not understand why I had to go back, but they let me go. That was love.

As I went through school, I did not have good friends after the two girls I played with moved away, except for a new friend I met in fourth grade, and stayed friends until our mid-forties. I played by myself. As I look back on my life, I look for the one person that was treating me special. Still, these people were usually a particular teacher or camp counselor, someone that was not permanent in my life. Some aunts and uncles were special, treated me like they loved me, and played with me.

But friends stopped being friends, and that wasn't easy. This continued to happen when I was an adult, and the feelings of abandonment were more pronounced as an adult. I felt hurt and lonely and not good enough. I was on 'guard' and not quick to share about myself, so people would tell me I was hard to get to know. But I needed to protect myself from being hurt. I became very sensitive.

Sometimes people would cancel plans, not come over or forget about having plans with me. I think now that I feared being rejected, so I was too cautious and kept people at a distance. I put walls up and did not let them in easily. But by the time I figured these out, it was a time in life when people already had their friends and groups, so it wasn't easy to make friends.

Eventually, I just became angry and hurt the more it happened. I became angry and did not even realize how it affected my speech, interactions, and ability to make and keep friends. This became an issue in my adult life and my work environment, and my business, along with difficulty with communication.

Not only did I have trouble contributing to groups, but the tone and attitude of my communication were an obstacle. I began to realize this when I was an adult, and after I did some deep inner work and worked with a coach. I was able to explore what was going on and fix it. This was a big step, and I felt relief and peace inside. I felt free to be myself, and if I did not make a friend or people said hurtful things to me, I could handle it most of the time. It is continuous and mindful work and not always comfortable.

I am grateful that I had work opportunities with colleagues who willingly initiated an effort to be my mentor and invest in my career. These nurses also became friends. Sometimes these women also said things that felt "mean" and "hurtful." The statements made me feel inferior, like I was not living up to their expectations. Also, they never explained their statements, so I just tried to make changes where I thought they were needed, and I missed what they meant.

I wanted to be friends because they were prominent in nursing. I learned a lot, personally and professionally, from being with them. I have to believe they mainly wanted to help me but didn't think they we being hurtful but tended to be a controlling type of personality. I think that was something I let happen to me because I was used to feeling like I was not good enough and as smart as them. I'm including some of my struggles.

At times it felt like I was being bullied and discriminated against. Still, I let it happen to me instead of overseeing myself and taking action because I didn't want to lose friends or lose them as friends.

A former nursing instructor was a long-time friend and someone I worked with, but she ended up dissolving the friendship. She invited me to accept a new position where she had started working in northern Michigan. After a few years, she told me I could not communicate with the staff. All I could figure out was that usually, I was direct and reported issues to staff without trying to beat around the bush. I tried being whom I was rather than sugarcoating. This fits with some of my feelings that people liked me initially but, after getting to know me, felt I was not quite good enough.

Late in our relationship, she told me, "You are too needy, Sheron." It came out of nowhere; I didn't say anything, and we continued our relationship, but it was not the same. I kept trying to please her and did things for her to help until she had another colleague to live with her. Then she stopped inviting me over for dinner or to go to the cabin. We often did big projects together that she wanted to do, like making soup or canning fruit and veggies.

Another time the person I thought was my best friend, we had been since the fourth grade, and now it was some 40 years, was visiting me in Traverse City. I had adopted my 13-year-old daughter and was settling in with her younger brother and sister. They were visiting their foster parents for the weekend, so she did not meet them.

In the meantime, my friend visited my oldest daughter, who lived a few streets away. When she returned, she said, "I don't think you should adopt the two small children; I don't think you can handle it." I don't know what conversation she had with my daughter, but her comments were exceedingly difficult to understand.

A year or so later, her daughter was getting married, and she called me and told me, "Don't bring the two kids to the wedding; enough kids are coming." Another time on the phone, she said we weren't best friends anymore. This was one of my most significant losses, and it took me years to let it go.

The people who said mean things to me didn't want to discuss or forgive me but just abandoned me as a friend. They were big losses. This was extremely difficult to take and left me feeling less worthy and empty inside. I felt like something was wrong with me. I was not good enough to be their friend, which decreased my self-esteem further. It seemed like it was often happening in my life, and I just kept stuffing it down and feeling worse and worse. I felt like I was trying to dig myself out of a deep hole, and when I got part way out, it happened again, and I fell back to the bottom. Maybe I was just trying to make something work and was not a good fit.

In retrospect, the comments and reasons I received might have been something I could have changed, but they also seemed like unfair assumptions that were caused by their own faults. If our friendships were valued, they would have worked through whatever their concern was.

The other factor may have been as many friendships do need to end because they were not healthy or serve either of us. Sometimes you can outgrow a friendship. I was seeing a therapist during these times, and perhaps I was changing because of that. I don't know the answer as to why these relationships did not survive, but these are my thoughts.

I loved my parents and knew that they did their best to raise me. I know that they had obstacles of their own as they were growing and affected how they navigated through their life. They were young, only 19 years old when I was born, and they both had losses in their childhood that were devastating. My mom was adopted and then lost both of her parents when she was young, by 16 years old. After that, she lived with guardians, which was not an ideal situation.

Dad lost his father when he was five years old, and his four brothers and one sister all had a part in raising each other. Neither of them outwardly experienced love from their parents, so they probably didn't know how to give it to me. In addition, they did not finish high school, and they moved our family to the

United States from Canada when I was five years old. This was a big change and made getting a job difficult. They had many obstacles to overcome.

They did not know how to help me when I was preparing to go on to nursing school, and they did not take me or go with me when I had interviews. They were proud of me. But when I went on to get my bachelor's and master's degrees, I heard comments like, "I don't know how you're going to pay for it," or "You don't need to be better than anyone else." They just did not understand. I learned to figure things out on my own.

All my stuffed feelings were whirling around in my head. I felt there was no room left to remember new information. I was having difficulty moving forward, and I wasn't sure who I was or wanted to be anymore. I needed clarity, and I couldn't progress without help. I was tired, overwhelmed, and unsure I was doing what I was supposed to do. My head felt like I had a cement block inside. My head felt heavy and like it was 'blocked up.' Without the help of my coach, I wouldn't be at the point where I know who I am or what I would like to do for the remainder of my life. Working with a coach and writing this book helped to bring everything together so I could plan to move along with my life.

Because of my experiences, I would make some suggestions for those who raise children.

My first suggestion to the reader is to show love freely and to teach the children about God and Jesus. Show them the difference when they have Jesus in their life. Talk to a local pastor to get help with this. You will observe a big difference in how your child behaves and responds to others. Our heart is the core of who we are, and when we ask Jesus to come into our heart, we have a 'beautiful' heart, and our life becomes a journey of the heart. Jesus is 'Light,' and we experience the 'Joy of the Lord' and can shine the Light of Jesus on others.

I know that no child should go through life thinking they are unloved. They are not deserving of the good things that God has provided for them. They should know they are unique and loved no matter what. God will never abandon them.

If you have any feelings such as mine, it might be helpful to seek out a coach to work with to gain clarity, purpose, and direction in your life. Also, it will be easier to know how to show them how much you love them because you love yourself. Each of us, including children, feel we are loved in different ways. Some feel they are more loved by receiving gifts, some by being physically touched, and some by hearing the word Gary Chapman, psychologist, and author, calls these 'words of affirmation.' Then the last two are to spend quality time with them and 'acts of service.'

If you are unsure what makes your child feel most loved, watch how your child reacts to times you think you are showing love or just ask him. Then simply show the child the way that means the most to him. Of course, we use all the ways, but the child's perception matters. That doesn't mean you stop doing the rest of them.

An example of each of the five love languages is:

Receiving gifts: this is clear but doesn't have to be large physical gifts all the time. Gifts can mean different things, like a loving note they find in their backpack, a new pencil, or a book. You can even teach the 'Gifts of the Spirit' and use them as examples of patience, knowledge, wisdom, giving, and teaching.

Physical touch: cuddle, hug, pat on the back, hold on your lap, kiss on the cheek, chase them, and play with them.

Hearing (words of affirmation): Tell them 'Out loud' you love them every day, tell them what a good job they did, tell them they are special, and they deserve that award. Let them know they don't have to be perfect just the best they can be, and that you and God love them just the way they are.

Spend quality time with them: have a date with one child at a time and do an activity of their choice. Don't be distracted by your phone or other things that come up.

Acts of Service: do something for them. Make a cake for them, make their bed for them.

Go out and shine your light for the children; take them and shine your light for others!

I have become a new me. I no longer have the anger I was showing. I have forgiven others and myself. I have forgiven my parents for not showing me their love knowing they did their best.

I realize that I am loved by God, and in Christ, God is my everlasting father. I am by no means finished working on myself, and old feelings resurface occasionally or more often recently as today, my confidence is increasing, as well as my self-worth and self-esteem. I seldom talk to myself negatively or call myself negative names. My 'inner critic' is not working overtime trying to convince me I'm no good.

I have worked for years building my relationship with God. I know He has been my protector, my father, my everything from the beginning, but I have felt Him in my life since I was 'Saved.'

He is love and showed me what it feels like. God doesn't just tolerate me; He's still working on me. He made me unique and created me for a purpose. He loves me just the way I am, imperfect.

SHERON CHISHOLM

"Freeing yourself was one thing, claiming ownership of that
freed self was another."

Tonia Morrison

5

LOSING MY FIRST LOVE

Healing Through The Guilt and Trauma of Suicide

"I have learned that it is your deepest pain that will empower you to grow into your highest self." Roxanne Naistus

I was 12 years old when my parents divorced, and my whole world changed. I went from living in the city with my entire family to traveling between my parent's homes 12 hours away from each other. My dad took me and my younger sister, and my mom took my brother and my older sisters.

Dad tried so hard and did such a good job of trying to raise us girls on his own.

I decided to move away from my dad and younger sister, who lived in Saskatoon, Saskatchewan, to Onion Lake First Nations north of Lloydminster, Saskatchewan. I wanted to live with my mother and three older sisters. I grew up in the city until I was 14 years old and now choose to live on the reserve. It took a while to get used to.

My parents (mom and stepdad) were very old-fashioned and lived a busy farm life, as well as traveling the rodeo trails. Mom always worked hard to provide.

It wasn't until I was 16 years old that I officially had a "boyfriend." I remember one time a boyfriend came to take me to a hockey game, and my stepdad and his rifle greeted him. So, needless to say, having a boyfriend was not easy.

Ferdinand was the one—my first love. We met up at a friend's house and began talking till dawn. Then he said, "I'm gonna come see you at your mom's." I thought to myself, yeah, right!! But then he did show up and told my parents he was there to buy eggs!

My parents would invite him in and have coffee and a visit. Then when he was finally done, we got a chance to have a quick visit. The charade only lasted a couple of times, but Mom knew.

The first time I invited Ferdinand into our home, my mother came into my room and shocked us both by saying, "Ok, if you two are going to be together, then Ferdinand, I am giving her to you! She is yours now," and walked out. This was an old Cree tradition, and one I guess that found me that day!

So then, the next thing I knew, he moved in with me, and we were officially "shacked up," as they say in the rez. Right from this point on, I knew that my time with Ferdinand would be short and, at times, difficult. He was so loving and caring and the best guy in the world. I was so completely in love with him.

However, I began seeing signs of possessiveness, insecurities, and so much grief, hurt, and anger. Ferdinand came into the relationship with lifelong pain and so much heartbreak from the past sexual and physical abuse he endured as a child and youth. He shared a lot of his trauma with me and as well as my mother. He struggled with this all his life. His pain and suffering at times were unbearable, and I was so young and did not know how to help him through this except just listen.

Naturally, a month after living together, I became pregnant with our first son. Ferdinand and I were extremely happy and excited to be expecting our first child. We decided to get our own place and moved into a basement suite in Lloydminster, Saskatchewan. I was 17 years old when we married, and my dad had to sign my marriage certificate. We wanted to be married before our baby came. Unfortunately, This is where I began to see just how dark things were going to get.

Whenever alcohol was involved, a different man would face me. One full of anger and aggression and physical and mental abuse. This was probably the first time he threatened to kill himself. He would tell me of all the previous attempts to take his life before meeting me. It made me so afraid. I never thought of leaving because he was all I knew, and I refused to break up our home for my son's sake.

Once I graduated high school, we packed the three of us up and moved to Edmonton, Alberta, where I tried to fulfill my dream of becoming a nurse at the University of Alberta. Unfortunately, it was at this time that my world halted and changed forever.

My son and I traveled to Onion Lake for Ferdinand's Mosom (Grandpa) wedding. April 1st, 1994. I remember this day so clearly. It was an early morning wake-up call to my mother's home. Ferdinand's brother called and screamed into the phone, saying, "Ferdinand is dead. He hung himself." I remember falling to the ground and my son running to me. We just sat there crying and screaming.

I was just a young woman, only 20 years old, with a two almost three-year-old son. I felt we were not enough to keep him here on this earth. I was numb and could not believe that it was happening.

The next few days were like a daze, and due to the circumstances, his family was upset with me. They blamed me. It was my fault he killed himself. I remember I was so destroyed inside that I could not fight and did not want to fight. I blamed myself.

I had no input in his funeral services, and everything that I placed in his coffin was taken out by his family and given to others. Thank God my parents and my family supported me and my son.

Inside, I thought to myself, well, you did it. You kept your word. You left me in a way that I would never recover. I was alone with my son. It was so hard, but I couldn't just roll up and die like I wanted to. I had to try to continue for my son. I promised no matter what, I would not ever leave him. I had my son to think of. He needed me.

I tried my hardest to go back to Edmonton and go back to school. But it got to be too much. I was grieving and struggling mentally with the loss of Ferdinand. My son and I moved back to Onion Lake. It was there that I decided to take away my pain and heartache by drinking and smoking marijuana and oh so many friends to party with.

I spent many years down this path. I found it easier to numb the pain than deal with anything. I remember many times breaking down and thinking I was no good, and then, at my lowest point, I attempted suicide myself. I figured my kids would be better without me. My reckless behavior continued to the point where I would lose my children if I did not get help. I hated to leave them, but I was destroying us and our home the way I was living.

I decided to place my oldest son with Ferdinand's mother and family. I was thankful they still wanted Randall to be a part of their family. My son was all they had left of Ferdinand. I knew he would be safe there. My other two children would go to my mother's. Then, I went to get help at Sandy Lake Healing Centre.

I was only to be there for 30 days; however, I was there for three months!!

I always tell people my time there was not only about my addictions. It was very much about dealing with all the trauma's that I had gone through. This was one of the hardest things to do, dealing with my grief and losses. Ferdinand was one of the many tragedies in my life. When I came home and got my kids back, I got a job at the band office. My kids and I got a small two-bedroom duplex at Onion Lake. The size didn't matter as long as we were all together. And we made it our home.

Eventually, we left Onion Lake in 2005 and moved to Lloydminster. My party days had started back up. I was still working but also drinking and smoking my pain away. I just could not deal with life.

It was not until 2010 that my life truly changed in the biggest way. I began a new way of life and started my true healing journey. I quit going out partying and began to see all the time I had wasted. Thank God my kids still loved me and forgave me. They never gave up on me. They were my rock.

My first granddaughter was born in 2010. I promised myself at that point that this life I was living must change. God blessed us with her for a reason. Slowly but surely, I made better choices. The hardest part was saying no to family and friends who still loved the party life.

It has been a long hard, healing journey, and now I am blessed with four children and six grandchildren. I've lived in our current home since 2010.

I did it! I created a safe environment for my grandchildren. Today, I run my own business from home called "Readings by Roxy" and am proud to say I have learned you can have many more positive memories by making better choices for myself and my family.

Suicide is something I do believe you never really get over. I lost my older sister to suicide as well. Because of the Energy Work I do and having an amazing mentor, I have found forgiveness and understanding towards Ferdinand throughout my healing journey. Because I know his full story, his spirit was broken as a child by the physical and sexual abuse endured by family members. He never got the opportunity to find his healing that he so needed. I am thankful to him daily for loving me and giving me my son, who has blessed us with four granddaughters. I still have love for him to this day. And it feels like just yesterday that he was here with us. It also has been challenging for my son to deal with losing his dad this way. Today we talk openly with my son and his daughters about their late "Mosom" (Grampa). I am thankful my son and now his girls have remained close to Ferdinand's family through the years.

I strongly encourage that if you have thoughts of hurting yourself, please reach out and get help. Alcohol and Drugs only make things worse. Please talk to someone and know that you are loved. Especially if you have children, they need you. The best version of you.

Thank you for reading my story. Hiy Hiy

ROXANNE NAISTUS

.

"We know that when a woman speaks truth to power, there will be attempts to put her down... I'm not going to go anywhere."

Maxine Walters

6

TRAUMA BOND

Recovering from Abuse and Healing Through Shadow Work

"One day, you will thank yourself for making the decisions that set you free." Unknown

To this day, I cannot explain what drew me to him. Maybe it was Kismet, and maybe it was just horrible luck. Little did I know it would turn out to be my foremost dream and worst nightmare all rolled into one. Funny how one swipe on my phone screen could land me on a two-year-long emotional roller coaster ride, concluding with a cataclysmic end in profound life lessons.

Bored one evening on my couch, feeling lonely, I was listlessly scrolling online when suddenly, there he was. Instantly I thought, "Who is THAT?! – I NEED to meet him!"

I mean, c'mon…his eyes, the muscles, that one cocked eyebrow. Definitely my "type." But there was something else…like an energetic pull that, to this day, I still can't put into words. I had no idea who he was, how old he was, where he lived, or if he was even single. So, as any resourceful female does, I snooped through his Instagram page in search of whatever info I could find. We started following each other, "hearting" each other's posts, and sending flirty fire emojis back and forth. Until one day, he posted a particularly alluring selfie, and I finally garnered the courage to send him a DM (direct message for those who aren't familiar with the online lingo).

"When do I get to see those gorgeous eyes in person?" I typed. I didn't have to wait long for a response: "Well, that's a very, very good start!" followed by a winking kiss emoji.

And so began a very, very eye-opening new chapter in my life.

My backstory…

I grew up an only child in Toronto, Ontario. My parents were typical middle-class parents; they did the best they could to provide for me, but I was left to my own devices to entertain myself. Before I turned 13, we moved half an hour east to Oshawa at the tail end of my grade 6 year. I wasn't the most popular kid in school, but I made friends easily. My parents didn't grant me as much freedom as some of my schoolmates, but I know now they were just trying to protect their little girl from the dangers of the streets.

I was more advanced than my classmates in my studies, but I refused to skip grade 7 because I wanted to stay in the same class as my new pals. I quickly bonded with a younger girl, Emmie, who lived across the street and became a rebellious teenager, sneaking out, smoking Rothman's cigarettes I had stolen from my father with my new bestie.

Emmie knew an older man who lived on the next street over from us in a rundown garage-like structure he called a house. She said he was a friend of her family (which consisted of her single absentee mother and delinquent older brother). She introduced me to this man, and we would visit him at his home, where he gave us candies, freezies and pop.

Soon I started visiting him on my own while I was walking our family dog. My parents of course knew nothing of this, or I would never have been allowed to go near his house. Being 13 and naïve, having never been exposed to anything potentially threatening, I believed he was just a nice lonely old man. He had never given me any reason to think otherwise. Until one day when I passed by his house, and he invited me in.

I told him I couldn't be there long, but he begged me to stay for a few minutes. He invited me to sit down on his bed and gave me a treat – I don't recall now what it was. After a while, my dog started getting antsy and I told him I needed to get home before my parents began wondering where I was. He wanted a hug before I left. I thought nothing of it because he always gave us girls hugs. Except this time, he held on longer than usual.

I've tried to push the memory of that day out of my head – I know now this is a coping mechanism of mine; to simply ignore things I don't want to think about – but what I do remember is that suddenly his hands were under my shirt, and he was kissing me. I was completely grossed out and started to panic.

He had me on his bed now and was laying on top of me, still trying to give me wet, slobbery kisses. His mouth was all over me and his fingers were trying to undo my pants. All I could think was, I need to get out of here. I pushed myself up from under him, hastily pulling my bra and shirt back down, and bolted out the door. I never went back. I didn't tell my parents or my friends what had happened. I felt embarrassed, ashamed, and just generally "icky" about it, so it was easier to simply not think about it at all.

Several months later, my parents were contacted by the police. It turned out he had done similar things to other young girls. They had found polaroid photos of at least 11 underaged girls in his home. I was called to testify in court.

What a horrendous ordeal for a young girl to go through. Luckily, I didn't end up testifying because he pleaded guilty before I was called to the stand. I followed behind my parents as we made our way out of the courtroom, and as my dad passed by where my perpetrator was sitting, he leaned over and whispered something to him. To this day I have no idea what he said but as any father would be towards someone who had molested his adolescent daughter, I'm sure it wasn't friendly. About a year later, we found out my assailant was deceased. We never mentioned it again.

I know my parents loved me, but I didn't really feel "seen" by them. I became an excellent student -- one of the top students in my class, actually -- and graduated high school with honors. I just didn't know what I wanted to do with myself career-wise. So, after my OAC year (grade 13 in Ontario), I ended up taking a year off to work and save up for college. I did the waitressing/bartending gig for a while but hated it. Eventually, I ended up going to college for Graphic Design and graduated with a diploma, but it just wasn't something I wanted to do with my life. I felt lost without a sense of direction or purpose.

Somewhere amid all of this, a mutual friend introduced me to my first long-term relationship partner, Mack. Aside from having a couple of boyfriends in junior and senior high, Mack was my first serious relationship.

Initially, I turned down his advances, but in time he won me over with his goofball sense of humor, athleticism, and irresistible smile. Mack had just joined the military right before we had started dating and left shortly thereafter for several months of basic training camp. We talked on the phone whenever he wasn't out in the field on training courses.

When he graduated from basic training, Mack got to choose three preferences for where he'd like to be posted to work. A colleague convinced him to pick Edmonton, Alberta because it was a "cool place to go." At this point, we were pretty smitten with each other, and he asked me to move across the country with him. Caught off guard, I panicked and said no.

As it got closer to the day he had to leave, I realized that my staying behind meant we would effectively be breaking up and going our separate ways. I started to think about all the "What Ifs." What did I really have in Oshawa that was so important? What if I regretted not going? Ultimately, I decided I didn't want to lose him and made the move.

I ended up getting a job at one of the gyms in Edmonton and was thriving, enjoying "adulting" with Mack in our newly renovated apartment on the north side of the city. I was making new friends and finally a decent paycheck. I was quickly promoted to Assistant Manager and in 2005 the owner of the gym offered me the opportunity to become the General Manager of the newest location, due to open at the end of the year. I would get to help build the new facility from the ground up.

The new club was my pride and joy. I had found my niche in the fitness industry! I even decided to try my hand at competing as a novice bodybuilder in the Figure category and absolutely fell in love with the sport, doing my first two shows in 2005 and 2006. Then, in 2007, Mack accepted an unexpected offer to be posted to Europe, so off we went to Germany for another adventure. We did a lot of traveling, took in many beautiful countries, and I made many more life-long friends. We adopted a 10-week-old English Bulldog there that we named Bella. Overall, it was an amazing experience that really matured me. But as many young "first-love" relationships go, we had our troubles. Mack and I split in 2010, and I was shipped home to Ontario. I was a mess.

There I was back home, in my early thirties, living with my parents, with no decent work prospects. I fell into a heavy depression, sleeping most hours of the day. I barely managed to drag myself to the gym a couple times a week. I started randomly having what I later learned were panic attacks, where I would lose the ability to focus my sight on any one object, and my heart would start to race. My whole body trembled, and I'd feel like I was going to faint. I felt so hopeless like I had nothing to live for. It was NOT where I thought I would be at that point in my life. I knew I had to take a leap of faith and venture back to Alberta, where at least I could get a better-paying job, be able to live on my own, and hopefully meet someone.

So, I packed up Bella, who was now a little over a year old, loaded up the Mazda 3 my dad had co-signed for me, and departed on a snowy Boxing Day morning, bound once again for Edmonton. A good friend from my old gym had a position waiting for me and another friend had agreed to rent me her old condo. I arrived on New Year's Day, 2011. Within a year I had an even better job working at a bank; something more stable that I could call a real career. My life was finally looking more promising.

Frustratingly, I was single for the next 11 years. 11 YEARS! I never imagined it would be that hard to find a relationship. The dating scene is a lot different now than it was when I was in college. I think social media is a major reason for this. I liken online dating to a sea of weeds one must claw their way through in meager hopes of finding that one hidden treasure at the bottom, trying not to drown in the process. Sure, I had plenty "situationships" (more than a casual dating encounter, but less than an actual relationship), some that lasted several months, most that ended in heartbreak or being "ghosted" (suddenly cut off with no communication or closure), but no official committed partners. Sadly, this is a common theme nowadays for most singles.

In March 2013, at 11 pm on a Sunday night, my phone rang. It was a long-distance call from my parent's landline. Given the time difference between Ontario and Alberta, my gut instantly told me it wasn't going to be good news. My parents wouldn't be calling me at that time on a Sunday unless something bad had happened.

When I answered, my mom, asked if I was alone and suggested that I sit down. She said there were a couple of police officers with her. Then her voice broke, and she cried, "Dad's gone." My father had suffered a massive heart attack, and paramedics weren't able to revive him. All I could say was, "Are you sure?". At that moment, I learned firsthand what genuine shock feels like. I vaguely remember one of the police officers asking if there was someone who could be with me so I wasn't alone. Of course, there wasn't.

After my father's passing, we decided my mother would move to Alberta to be closer to me.

My mental health was failing. On a Thursday afternoon, after a particularly grueling day at work, I had a full-blown panic attack. Sitting at the desk in my office, trying to calm myself down, my mom suddenly texted me: "Can you please pick up milk on your way home from work?"My heart pounding, I replied, "Umm actually, I think I need to go to the hospital. Can you please come get me?"

She immediately called me. "What's going on?" she asked. I said, "I think I'm having a panic attack. Can you please come take me to the hospital? I can't drive right now."

Nine hours later, I had a prescription for Ativan and a referral to see a psychiatrist. I took a leave of absence from work. After three sessions, the psychiatrist diagnosed me with "situational anxiety disorder," meaning that my stressors were external but persistent and thus had taken a toll on my nervous system over time. He further referred me to a social worker. She was very kind and empathetic and a good listener, but beyond that couldn't help me within her scope of abilities, so she referred me to a Cognitive Behavior Therapist. She was much more impactful for me. Over several months of seeing her, she taught me to think differently about how I reacted to certain negative situations.

However, I still wasn't in a good place mentally despite all the therapy sessions. I was once again battling depression and physical side effects from my anxiety disorder. Those who have never dealt with this may not understand it. I had people say, "Stop overthinking," or "Don't worry so much. Everything will work out." I know they meant well, and in the grand scheme of things, my situation could have been much worse. I like to think I'm a strong person, and for the most part, I am, but even the strong ones have cracks in their armor. I am my father's daughter, stubborn as hell on the outside but secretly suffering in silence on the inside.

I had always felt like my brief stint in bodybuilding was unfinished business. Competing was the one thing I have ever done that was 100% for myself. I am endlessly fascinated with the science of nutrition and how food can affect the body to such a precise degree in conjunction with exercise. The mechanics of weightlifting and the body's response to manipulating macronutrients and water just "click" for me.

So, I decided to finish what I had started -- I had a point to prove to myself and to anyone who doubted me.

My first regional show back on the scene was in June 2017. I just missed placing in the top five, which was required to move on to the provincial level. Truth be told, I was pretty disappointed, but realistically I knew I had a lot of catching up to do. There was another regional show coming up that October, and I told my coach I was going for it.

I will never forget Saturday, October 7th, 2017. The competition was fierce that day. I was competing in two categories: Master's Figure and the Open "Tall-D" Height class. The Master's category went first. After performing our mandatory posing for the judges, we waited anxiously, each of us silently praying to be called back to the stage as one of the top five chosen finalists. I was nervous. Really nervous. After everything I'd been through in the past few years, I NEEDED this. In fact, I'd never wanted anything so badly in my life and couldn't handle another disappointment. Closing my eyes, I discreetly crossed my fingers at my sides and listened to the competitor numbers being called out by the emcee.

With each of the first four call outs, my heart sank a little bit more, but then I heard it, "…competitor #70."

I did it! I made the top five! Trying not to stumble in my five-inch stiletto heels -- I am NOT graceful when wearing heels higher than three inches -- I took my place on the last "X" taped on the stage floor and immediately went into my front pose. I could feel my cheek twitching as it always does when I'm nervous (the stage still scares the hell out of me to this day), and tried to smile even though my lips were sticking to my dehydrated gums.

Each placing was called in ascending order. Not once did it cross my mind that I might actually win, so when the presenter placed a silver medal around the runner-up's neck, I stood there, stunned, trying to process what had just happened. I WON!!! At 39 years old, I was now standing in the coveted "Center Stage" position. The last woman standing.

So many emotions swept over me: shock, happiness, pride, and gratitude. But mostly *validation*. Finally, I'd proved to myself that I had what it took to succeed at something.

I advanced all the way to Nationals, and on Saturday, August 3rd, 2019, the impossible happened. I earned the title of Overall Division Champion and was awarded my Pro Card as an IFBB Elite Pro Athlete. It was the proudest day of my life.

Sadly, a few weeks later, I was hit with another devastating blow. My beloved Bella, who had been by my side for over a decade, became seriously ill. I racked up my credit card trying to save her, but my efforts were futile. I had to make the heartbreaking decision to put her down. Anyone who knows me knows how much I loved that dog. She was my sidekick, my best friend. It seemed like whenever something good happened in my life, something terrible followed.

Then came 2020, the year that changed just about everyone's life. That's when I met HIM.

And then there was Johnny....

My online flirting game with Johnny had been going on for a while, but we just couldn't seem to match up our schedules to meet in person. Finally, in early February, he agreed to come over to my house. (Note: I am fully aware it is not the best idea to invite someone I haven't met to my house. However, I had no reason to think that he posed a threat. Besides, I was too excited.)

Johnny was super late arriving at my place for someone who lived only minutes away. When he finally pulled up, I opened the garage door to let him park inside out of the snow. The first words out of his mouth were, "Oh my God, you're pretty."

One thing about me: I've always had strong intuition. I have an uncanny ability to read people's energy without consciously trying to. It's just a gut feeling I get from being in someone's presence, even for a few minutes. In fact, I've given people chills with my knack for picking up on sketchy vibes from people who otherwise seem harmless. And at that moment, my spidey senses went into overdrive.

My first thought was he was either high, intoxicated, or both. He hadn't said anything alarming, but something in the tone of his voice had started my heart racing. I suddenly felt panicked and disappointed at the same time.

He made himself right at home almost immediately, hopping up on my kitchen counter and observing me closely while he chatted animatedly. I ordered a pizza in hopes that if I got some food into him, he would sober up enough to drive home. I should have sent him home afterward, but I didn't. As he became more clearheaded, I started making excuses for him in my head; maybe he was just nervous and had a few drinks or smoked some weed before he came over. It had happened with dates in the past. In any case, he was starting to become calmer and more appealing. He was quite attractive and fit too. I made the grave mistake of letting him stay over, and I'm sure you can guess what ensued.

Over the course of the next couple of months, we hung out more often. My initial impression of him faded like a distant memory. The fast pace of our relationship was obviously a red flag, but I didn't care. I was having fun. Not even two months into dating, he "accidentally" let the L-word slip out. He jokingly laughed it off but asked me where I stood with our relationship, whether I felt we should be exclusive or keep casually dating. I told him I'd like to be exclusive as a committed relationship was my goal, and he enthusiastically agreed. He told me he was excited for a "fun life with me." I understand now that he was love-bombing me, but at the time, I was so happy I overlooked it.

One thing that did weigh on my mind was his drinking. He was plowing through a 750ml bottle of hard liquor every 2-3 days and often drove under the influence. On one occasion, he backed into my garage and hit the shelving unit I had in the corner, breaking one of the shelves and toppling it over, spilling numerous items onto my garage floor. The next morning he simply stepped over it and left without even offering to help clean up the mess or replace the broken shelf.

My gut kept telling me something wasn't adding up. As much as I tried to ignore it, I felt Johnny was hiding something from me. One weeknight at the end of March, I had to work the next morning while he began days off from his job as a paramedic, so we went to be early. He was so drunk that he got up, walked around to my side of the bed, and proceeded to urinate all over my mattress and fabric bed frame. I tried to stop him and direct him to the bathroom, but he was completely out of it. He simply went back to his side of the bed, climbed back under the covers, and was instantly dead asleep again.

During my frantic effort to get the bedsheets off before the wetness soaked through, something in me snapped. This was NOT normal behavior for a 37-year-old grown man. Spotting his phone plugged in on the bedside table, I snatched it and went downstairs. I had seen him swipe his passcode enough times that I knew I could probably get it right within the allotted three tries before it locked me out.

I'm not normally the type of woman to go through my partner's phone, but my instincts were screaming at me that I would find something there that I deserved to know.

Within seconds I was reading sickening conversations with multiple women and one very questionable convo with a male "friend." He was sending selfies to other girls while he was at work, often sending the same pics to numerous people. Some of them had been taken in my home gym, and he was pretending it was his buddy's house! In every conversation, it was as if he was playing a role, acting like a totally different person in each one.

I thought if I kick him out in the morning, he was just going to continue deceiving everyone else. So, I copied every phone number from every conversation I deemed inappropriate, and I sent a group text. It went something like this:

"My name is Leticia, and I'm Johnny's girlfriend. He is passed out drunk in my bed right now after having urinated on it. I got into his phone. He has been cheating on me with multiple women and is also lying to all of you. From one woman to another, I thought you should know."

Despite the early hour of the morning, it didn't take long for the messages to pour in. Most of the women were appalled and thanked me for letting them know. Several told me how sorry they felt for me and assured me I was brave for outing him. Some admitted they suspected something was up with him and thanked me for the confirmation. One woman was particularly outraged, as she had been under the impression that she was in a relationship with him too. They had met around the time he and I had.

It just blew my mind! How did he keep up with so many stories? How did he even find the time to do all of this? Now I knew why he slept with his phone underneath his pillow most nights and always took it to the bathroom with him. I was embarrassed and felt so stupid. Why did I ignore the signs? And worse, was there no one left out there who was honest and loyal?

A few hours later, I woke him up. I told him I had outed him to every one of his "girlfriends" and not-so-politely told him to get the (bleep) out of my house. At first, he acted like he didn't understand until I read his own texts back to him. Then he burst into tears. He claimed he "wasn't sure if we would last, so he had to have backups." He talked in circles, most of it just word salad. He was furious with me for exposing him and "ruining his life," yet he refused to leave. It took a couple of hours, but I finally got him out. I did not go to work that day.

He went home and immediately started drinking. My phone was blowing up with texts and calls from the woman who thought she was Johnny's girlfriend but now realized she was the "other woman," as well as a couple of girls he had known for years. Meanwhile, he continued to ream me out for exposing him.

Playing the victim, Johnny threatened to commit suicide and ended up being held overnight in the hospital. I was hesitant to talk to him, but I started to feel sorry for him. It dawned on me that something must've happened to him to make him this way. Not that that was an excuse for his behaviors, but I recognized the signs of internal struggle. I knew from my own battles with depression what it felt like to be alone. I also knew that the worst thing that could happen to someone in his state of mind would be for the person closest to him to abandon him. That person was me.

Sometimes empathy can be a curse.

Johnny chose to designate me as his emergency contact. When the hospital called to confirm my information, I asked that the attending psychiatrist call me. We had a lengthy discussion about what had transpired. He was quite concerned for my personal safety and advised me to keep an overnight bag packed in my car in case I had to get away from him. It was this psychiatrist who first mentioned the word "narcissism" to me. I had a vague understanding of what narcissism was, but I had never personally experienced it on any significant level.

It has taken a long time to forgive myself for taking Johnny back that night. There are some who simply cannot understand it and may even think less of me for doing so. However, many of those individuals have never been in the same position.

Writing this chapter now, knowing how many people will read it, brings up such overwhelming feelings of anxiety and shame. If you had told me a year prior that I would give a cheater another chance, I'd have laughed because cheating was something I would never tolerate. It's more complicated than that, though; I had true feelings for him, and that doesn't just turn off automatically. Plus, manipulators are skilled at what they do, especially when they've been doing it for years.

I was the perfect victim because although I didn't know what Johnny's trauma was, I understood there was a root cause for his behavior, and it was in my nature to help others. I also believed that he had real feelings for me, despite what he was doing behind my back. Another significant factor was I had developed co-dependency attachment issues from my childhood. Like him, I was scared to be alone. On the surface, Johnny gave me everything I had always longed for.

I gave Johnny an ultimatum; I told him I'd give him another chance, but I had a list of requests. I wanted him to change his phone number, delete his social media accounts, stop drinking, and seek therapy. To my surprise, he agreed and did what I had asked him to do. Sort of.

The rest of 2020 was a bumpy ride. I caught him texting women again and again I gave in after he begged me for forgiveness when I threatened to leave. However, it was more minimal each time and eventually seemed to stop altogether. For several months our relationship seemed to be going well. I became close with his family, attending various functions and holiday gatherings. I grew to love him more than anything and was fully invested in our relationship, but eventually, negative things started happening again.

He replaced the whiskey with vodka seltzers and added other substances. We had a vigorous sex life, but when he was drinking and/or high he often became too rough. One night he body-slammed me to the floor in front of his fridge, bouncing my head off the floor. Pinning me, he put his hands around my throat and pretended to choke me, but he squeezed too hard, and I started to cough, struggling to get air. When I protested, he reached over and rammed the freezer door against the side of my head three times, damaging my ear drum. I had pain in my left ear for days afterward. On another occasion, he thought it would be funny to hit me with a metal police baton that he kept in his car, leaving two stinging welts across my thigh.

I blamed the physical abuse on the alcohol because he never remembered it the next day and always went back to treating me with affection.

In July 2020, on his way to meet me at our campground for the weekend, Johnny was pulled over by the RCMP and issued a DUI. We had a volatile argument that night, and afterward, he admitted that he "didn't know why he was doing these things."

After his DUI, Johnny seemed to settle down, and our relationship grew surprisingly peaceful. For the rest of 2020 and half of 2021, there were no signs of cheating. Although he was still using substances, he hadn't been inebriated, and he no longer physically hurt me. We talked about selling our houses and buying one together. I wanted to compete one more time, so we both booked a week off work that November to go to Mexico, where I planned to compete at the Cancun Pro show. If the show was canceled due to Covid, we would at least have a vacation.

Afterward, we were going to start trying for a baby. We adopted a gorgeous 10-month-old American Bulldog and began raising him together. We were a happy little family with big plans. I thought the worst was behind us.

Just before my birthday in June of 2021, we went to Banff for the weekend. I was in the kitchenette of our hotel room, putting dinner together after a pleasant day of hiking. Johnny was on the balcony smoking a mini cigar, playing Clash Royale on his phone. Our pup was enjoying a stuffed toy on his bed, waiting for me to toss him some leftovers, when I received a text from one of my girlfriends. She asked if Johnny and I were ok. I told her we were great, we were in the mountains and asked why she was inquiring.

She had matched with him on Tinder (an online dating site) and had been talking to him for about two weeks, trying to gauge if it was him or someone using his photos. She sent me screenshots of the entire conversation. My internal alarms were ringing off the hook. Not again! Why? We've been so good! Feeling that familiar sickness in my stomach, I asked him about the profile, and as expected, he denied it. He claimed it was one of the girls who was upset that we were still together and had been trying to break us up. To be honest, it did seem like that could be a possibility, and I couldn't prove otherwise, so I let it go even though I knew the truth.

After yet another suspicious incident the following month, I demanded we go to couples counseling. It was my last-ditch effort to salvage what was left of our relationship. At our last session, our psychologist asked Johnny what his biggest fear was. In tears, he told her his biggest fear was losing me.

In late August 2021, everything came to a head. I had organized a birthday outing for him and some of our mutual friends at a local restaurant/cigar lounge. We had a great meal. He enjoyed a birthday cigar, we took lots of photos and went home happy. I had to work the next morning while Johnny had the day off. He had started taking Fridays off a couple of weeks prior to use up his remaining vacation time.

My intuition was still nagging me, so I purchased a small GPS tracker – perfect for hiding in a vehicle. Johnny was driving my SUV with a suspended license; therefore, I had a right to know where he was taking it. The tracker linked to an app on my phone that would notify me when my SUV was moving and showed me on a map exactly where it was parked.

The morning after his birthday, Johnny texted to let me know he was running out to buy dog food. The app showed me he was parked in the plaza where the pet store was. About an hour or so later, he was back home again. So far, so good! Later that afternoon, while working on a report, my app suddenly alerted me that my vehicle was on the move again. Curious, I kept an eye on it for a while to see where he ended up. Johnny had parked in a residential area, in front of an unfamiliar address, approximately halfway between our two neighborhoods.

It wasn't his parents' house. Wasn't his aunt's house either. And I was pretty darn sure it wasn't where his brother lived. "Well, maybe he's picking up something he bought online," I thought. Let's test that theory…

"How's the day, babe?" I texted.

"Oh good, was just playing Rainbow 6. I'll probably take the dog for a walk soon. I think he wants to go out." Johnny replied.

"Aww, nice. Take a pic of him for me." I said, calling his bluff. He was implying that he was at home playing online with his friends, and our dog was with him.

"Ok, I'll do that after I get back from Walmart. I need a few things, and I wanted to look for a game for us to bring camping next weekend." Strange, how did he go from being at home about to walk the dog to being on his way to Walmart? He was always the worst liar. I couldn't believe he still thought I was that gullible. I knew I had to get to the address on the tracker immediately, so I jumped in his car, determined to catch him red-handed this time.

Sure enough, there was my SUV parked in front of some stranger's house. I parked his car a couple of houses down and texted him again.

"Are you still at Walmart? Could you grab something for me while you're there?"

"Yup" was his reply. I called his phone immediately, but it went to voicemail. There was a reason he wasn't answering it. I got out of his car and walked over to check on my SUV. Peeking inside, I noticed an empty vodka cooler in my console, still wet around the opening. He had been drinking while driving my vehicle. My nerves frazzled, I approached the front door of the house.

As I walked up to the door, I noticed there was a doorbell camera, so I put my hand over it while I rang the bell. A female voice answered in a blatantly mocking tone, "Why are you hiding the camera?"

"Is Johnny there?" I asked pointedly.

"Whooooo?" she crooned.

I repeated myself again, more firmly this time. "Is JOHNNY there?" I didn't stop ringing the doorbell.

There were two large Boxers in the front bay window, barking madly. I could hear shuffling and whispering on the other side of the door, but no one came out. After a couple of minutes, the doorbell suddenly stopped working. They had shut it off from the inside.

Furious, I texted Johnny again. "Are you going to come outside, or are you going to hide like a coward?" No reply.

"Johnny, I want the keys to my vehicle. I suggest you come out here and give them to me, or I'm going to call the police. Seeing as you've been drinking and driving with a DUI, I don't think that's going to end well for you."

The next thing I knew, Johnny was on the sidewalk behind me, tears already welling up in his eyes.

"Why are you stalking me?" he whined.

"At Walmart, huh? Riiight. Give me my keys." I put my hand out, waiting for him to hand them to me, but he didn't move.

"I don't know why you're stalking me! I was just about to go to Walmart. I was dropping something off to my buddy Jayden first. Why are you being like this?" he cried.

"That's funny because I literally just asked if you were STILL at Walmart, and you said YUP. I'm not stupid. Who's the girl Johnny?" He looked down at the sidewalk. No acknowledgment whatsoever. "Give me my keys." I repeated.

He started to pull them out of his pocket and then offered up another twist to his story. "I was about to go to Walmart. I didn't know I had to report to you everywhere I go. I was just playing R6 with Jayden. He lives in the basement."

"WHO'S THE GIRL?!?" I shouted. I had had enough of the lies and crocodile tears.

"Give me my car keys then," he said as I took my SUV's fob from his hand. Turning, I quickly tossed his keys into the bushes a couple of houses down. I knew I had to get back to his house, grab my stuff and our dog, and get out before he beat me there. He looked like a bewildered child as he wandered off to fetch his keys.

I had never been so distraught/angry/humiliated in my entire life! Something in me snapped. As I turned to run to my SUV, I stopped for a second, picked up a small rock from the garden bed, and hurled it through her front window. I guess I felt like she deserved to suffer that small pain for enabling Johnny's infidelity. I'm not proud of it to this day, but I've since learned there's a term for my reaction; it's called "Reactive Abuse" – when a victim of abuse has been pushed to breaking point and lashes out in frustration.

Racing Johnny back to the house, I called the police. I explained what had happened, that he had been drinking, and that there would likely be an altercation. He beat me by seconds and locked the gate so I couldn't get in. Desperate to get our dog, I scrambled over the fence and let myself in with my copy of his house key.

While I frantically collected my belongings, he tried every immature tactic he could think of to stop me from leaving, including stashing my coat in the washing machine. While I retrieved it, he hid our dog's leash in an ottoman and sat on it. I pushed and shoved, but I couldn't move him. He just sat there, eyes glazed, not saying a word. Giving up, I grabbed our pup by the collar and lead him into the back of my SUV. On my way out the door, I turned and said, "I'll never understand why you did this to us."

For the next few months, Johnny desperately tried to win me back. He love-bombed me harder than ever. Claimed he was having nightmares and throwing up. He bought tickets for us to go on a Halloween hike, and I stupidly went, hoping he was feeling true remorse. (FYI, there's a big difference between remorse and regret.) He finally put away the pile of laundry on the floor that I had always hounded him about and sent me pictures of his freshly cleaned house to show that he was "trying."

One evening he offered to make me dinner and asked me to bring our dog because he missed him. He even dressed up. While watching a movie afterward, he ran upstairs to change, and I quickly used the bathroom. That uncanny intuition of mine prompted me to look in the garbage can beside the toilet. I found several tampon wrappers, indicating a female had been in his house, likely for several days. He claimed they belonged to his friend Jim's wife, Halley. More lies. That's when I finally walked out his door for good.

The entire time, he had still been seeing the woman from the mystery house (not to mention a few others). Within weeks, he announced that he was in a relationship with her. Within weeks of that, she was pregnant. A mutual friend confirmed she was indeed the same woman who lived at the house I had caught him at that awful day. For months, he had been telling her he was single, and when I showed up at her door, he told her, "Don't open the door. That's my crazy ex!" After I left, he ran a smear campaign on me, telling the few allies he had (who don't know me) that I was unstable. Meanwhile, another woman he had tried to cheat with came forward and described how he had physically assaulted her for refusing to sleep with him. Unreal.

Johnny left me with C-PTSD. I've had many months of therapy since with two wonderful psychologists, one of whom specializes in Narcissistic Personality Disorder. I became consumed with studying NPD. The more I learned about it, the more it resonated: his love-bombing, future-faking, gaslighting, lying, cheating, and triangulation with other "supplies." With every survivor's story, I read, I had déjà vu remembering something Johnny had done, the behaviors identical. It is common for someone with NPD to also have other mental illness(es), as I suspect that Johnny does.

Therapy and research helped me immensely in my healing journey, as well as supportive friends. C-PTSD is no joke, no matter what the cause is. For months, I cycled through periods of sadness, anger, and numbness. I berated myself daily for not walking away earlier. I couldn't fathom how he could say he loved me, then do the things he was doing behind my back. I now know that this is what a "trauma bond" is; the attachment an abused person feels for their abuser, much like Stockholm syndrome. Ultimately, I had to go within. I couldn't change what had happened, so I had to change myself.

Therapy helped me to recognize and work through my co-dependency issues and my desperate "need" for a partner. I had allowed Johnny to hurt me because I didn't want to be alone.

Betrayal aside, he had given me the affection and attention I didn't have as a child. He gave me a sense of security because I knew he wouldn't leave me like others had left me. I yearned to fix in him what I had never fixed in myself.

I embarked on a spiritual journey, studying reiki, meditation, sound baths, and other natural healing modalities. Then I had an epiphany: I could use my knowledge of fitness and nutrition, mental health, and spirituality to help others –– not only in recovering from toxic relationships but also in doing the inner shadow work for optimal wellness. I can use my passion for coaching and writing to inspire others to live their best lives.

As for me, I've forgiven myself. I've forgiven Johnny too. Not for the things he did (because those things are truly inexcusable), but for being who he is. I've accepted what happened had nothing to do with me and everything to do with his own internal struggles. Unfortunately, he will continue to repeat his behaviors no matter who he is with. I have no regrets; I only feel sorry for him. He will never know what true love feels like, and that is sad.

My relationship with Johnny taught me some valuable lessons:

- To let go of my need for revenge; karma will take care of that.
- To let go of the past and practice the art of being present in the "now."
- To set healthy boundaries for myself and uphold them in future relationships.
- To face my fear of being alone and to become whole without depending on someone else.

- To control my own responses to triggers, understand I cannot control the actions of others.
- To trust my intuition because it has never steered me wrong.
- To honor my self-worth and never again settle for less than I deserve.

I didn't know then what I was dealing with, but now I am well-versed in personality disorders. At the end of the day, the terminology doesn't matter; manipulation is NOT okay. When someone repeats the same harmful behavior over and over, trust that it's not a mistake. It's a choice being made intentionally without remorse. I recognize now when someone is choosing to act poorly from a place of internal trauma. The empathetic part of me still tries to help, but I know when to walk away. Some people cannot be helped…let them play out their own fate.

I will always speak my truth because, in the end, truth always wins. If my story helps even one person gather the strength to leave a toxic situation, then it was worth being vulnerable. Remember: healing is not a destination. It's a perpetual voyage.

LETICIA RODRIGUEZ

If you are currently in a relationship with an abusive partner or feel your well-being is in danger, leave if you can and go no-contact. Document everything and keep evidence. Find safe shelter with friends/family. Report your situation to authorities, seek help from a professional, and most importantly: stay no contact!

"I'm tough, ambitious, and I know exactly what I want. If that makes me a bitch, okay."

Madonna

7

THE GOLDEN YEARS
FORGIVENESS ISN'T PRETTY

"Never does the human soul appear so strong as when it forgoes revenge." Edwin Hubbel Chapin, Poet

Mom was the trailblazing Boomer. She was the first woman in our neighborhood to divorce and let her child come home from school with a key around her neck. Mom was an independent woman who didn't need a man. She could do it all until she couldn't.

I was 50 years old and should have seen the signs. I hoped Mom's frequent phone calls meant she had more interest in me. I thought there was a light at the end of the tunnel. I thought maybe, she started to see me.

"Hey, Mom, what's up?" I was cheery to see her call first. That rarely happened.

"I can't get on the internet. My router went out. I called the company. I have to use this brand, but Best Buy doesn't have it. I don't know what I'm going to do. I have to get back to a lady about a horse, but I don't have her number. I only talk to her on Facebook. I'm here in the parking lot and…"

She sounded all over the place.

"Wait, Mom. What parking lot are you in?"

"I'm at Best Buy. I need a new router. I told you that. Aren't you listening? But they don't have one. None of the customer service people want to help. This lady may sell the horse. And it's Saturday. If I don't contact her by tomorrow, she might sell the horse. I'm standing in the parking lot. I don't know what to do."

I'd never heard my mother flustered. How did she not know what to do? An alarm went off, like when you feel someone is trying to scam you, but you don't know how.

"Mom, maybe somewhere else has it. Give me the model number. I'll look it up."

"Hurry up. It's already 5 o'clock. These stores are going to close."

"It looks like there's a newer model over at…"

"You aren't listening. It has to be this model. It won't work with any other one. You aren't any help at all."

"Hold on. There's another location not too far from you."

I texted her with the next possible purchase point and told her to call me later. She didn't call and never answered her phone that evening. Not unusual.

I waited until Sunday evening to call again. She didn't remember our conversation the day before. She recounted the drama of Best Buy, the router, and how she finally found one. Thank goodness because she could talk to the lady about another horse. It was like I was talking to a different person.

As soon as I hung up, I called Lois. She was the only friend Mom had who would know what was going on.

"Lois, I was talking to Mom. She doesn't sound right. Is everything ok?"

"She's been having problems for a while now. I finally convinced her to go to the doctor. There's an appointment for an MRI next week. I told her I'd take her because she was nervous. The follow-up is the week after." Lois said.

Mom never said anything to me about an MRI. Nothing about Lois convincing her to go to the doctor. No mention of why she felt the need to go.

"You can't ever tell your mom I told you this. She would never forgive me. She'll never trust me again." Lois said.

Mom had been getting confused, having panic attacks, and forgetting things. Maybe just old age. Maybe something else.

"I'm getting on a plane to come out there after the MRI. Don't tell her I'm coming," I said.

I showed up a week later on Mom's doorstep unannounced. That would be a normal or pleasant surprise for some families. Not for my mom. Any visit of any kind was an invasion of her privacy and personal schedule. So when I knocked on the door, I should have gotten a good lecture on how she wasn't expecting me. She should have waved me away or at least complained I was there.

"Oh, hi," Mom said as she unlocked the screen door.

Her eyes said everything. She thought she'd forgotten and tried to pretend it was normal.

We had an uncomfortable but pleasant conversation, and she never asked me why I was there or for how long. I left a couple of hours later to stay with a friend. There was never a time I was welcome to stay at my mom's house. It was too "disruptive to my schedule," according to her.

I came to see her every morning. It took Mom three days to get the courage to ask why I'd come.

"I'm going to the follow-up visit with you for the MRI," I said.

"I don't need you going to the doctor with me. That's ridiculous. Go home."

"No, Mom. You need someone with you. Whatever the doctor says, we need to research it. You know I'm good at that."

I'd never stood up to my mom before. I'd never insisted on anything. But her weakness emboldened me. I couldn't leave without knowing what was happening. God knows she'd never tell me.

After the follow-up appointment, I called my husband.

"I just dropped Mom back home. We need to talk."

"Ok, talk." He said, slightly irritated at my tone.

"Mom has vascular dementia. There is no cure. It will only get worse. She's a menace to herself living alone with those animals."

"That doesn't sound good." He said tentatively.

"I need to move out here. I need to take care of her."

Those words hung in the air. Like wet wool hanging to dry.

"Why do you think you have to take care of her? She beat the shit out of you as a kid. She's never cared about you."

"Because there's no one else to do it. She's going to start the place on fire, or the damn horse is going to trample her. She isn't good. She's changing. I can see it."

"You don't owe her anything."

"I know. It's not that. I just need to do it. I need to be better to her than she was to me."

"So are you asking me or telling me? You also haven't said anything about me going with you."

"I have to do this. I'd like you to come, but if you can't, I understand. I have to do it, with or without you."

"Ok, I guess we're moving to Utah."

Within weeks, we downsized, packed a U-Haul, and settled into a small 2-bedroom apartment five minutes from Mom's house.

I spent time researching dementia, new drugs, and natural supplements. I quickly took over making appointments with specialists and testing. Mom kept a calendar on her counter with daily notes and things to remember. We had a system.

Only a few months later, Mom was coughing more than usual. Her legs swelled up, and she didn't have energy. Her phone rang busy all morning. I drove over. She was sitting outside on a chair and couldn't get up. She had the phone and the old yellow pages in her lap.

"Mom, what's going on?" I said. She had a dazed look.

"I'm trying to find a doctor to get me an appointment today. I don't feel right. Everyone's booked, don't bother me. I have to find one."

"Why didn't you call me?"

"You aren't a doctor, are you? What are you going to do?"

I called her primary physician, who told me to take her to the hospital.

At the emergency room, they determined congestive heart failure. Mom spent a week in the cardiac unit and went home in better spirits than I'd ever seen her. It was as if the more her brain deteriorated; the more her emotional walls came down. It was the first time she allowed people to take care of her. She was kind to the staff and gentle with me.

After the heart failure, we had at least three appointments a week. I had to start regulating medicines. We had a system for everything, and bright post-it notes reminded her of the systems. It all worked for a while.

As I focused on the regimented schedule for Mom, a caldron boiled through my guts and overflowed into my subconscious. I was having panic attacks, and driving around my hometown triggered PTSD. Doctor appointments for Mom became difficult.

"You're very lucky to have a great daughter looking after you, Rose." The doctors said to Mom.

"It's been nice. We've been renewing our friendship." Mom said.

I wanted to scream at the doctors. Tell them how she used to beat me with horse whips and rip my clothes off so I wouldn't run away. I wanted to say how delusional she was, and we were never friends, but I smiled like the good girl she taught me to be.

I kept reminding myself: I was doing this because I was a good person, not because she was.

Most people become more angry and irritable as dementia progresses. Mom became more docile, childlike, likable, and fun. We laughed, stopped for her favorite donuts, and she told stories about her childhood. I learned things she'd never talked about before. She became more human, more womanly, and less of her battle ax persona.

I understood why she became a calcified, fiercely solitary person. She was damaged so many times. Fury was the only tool she had. I started to have compassion for her, but forgiving and forgetting are separate actions.

Late in the summer, we took Mom to her last horse show, and after stopping for ice cream. God created a fiery sunset I'll never forget. It matched the flames I felt inside. We sat on the terrace admiring the divine handiwork, and something in the warm summer air inspired Mom to tell my husband about her life while I was growing up.

I couldn't look at her while she was talking. If pain and acidic rage could ooze out of the skin, my chair would have dissolved underneath me.

In her story, she was a heroine. She did everything independently and fought the men who tried to stop her. She worked tirelessly for her goals and spent most of her free time with friends riding horses in the mountains and gullies. She was a pioneer woman for her age group. The patriarchy or her unruly children were not going to stop her.

At that moment, all the pieces of my life came together.

My parents divorced when I was seven. They adopted my brother and me because having children was something you're 'supposed to' do. After the divorce, the children were inconvenient extra pieces in the new puzzle. Children only fit in with marriage and family life. Now Mom wanted to live the horsewoman's dream; wild and free, alone on a ranch. However, she couldn't give us back, and she'd never endure the shame of giving us up.

So we became her noose and slaves.

While she pictured herself as a wonder woman, I cared for my little brother, cooking, cleaning, minding all the animals, and getting the whip when it wasn't up to standard. While she was going to school, working full time, and using weekends to ride horses with friends, I was sexually abused by neighbors and scrounged through cabinets to find extra food because I was chronically hungry.

We, the ungrateful minions, should have bowed down and given homage. All I remember was being alone most waking hours and nonstop screaming and beating when she was home. No wonder why we couldn't concentrate at school and earned inconsistent grades.

That evening of ice cream, sunset, and story, I chose silence as the high road. We drove Mom home as the horizon lost its glory.

The next day I watched Mom from across the room. She was becoming more feeble. She needed more and more help. I had to wrangle her into doing what she needed to do. It was a constant dance of repeating things and trying not to be annoyed.

Then the thought came: I could hurt her. I could hurt her and pay her back. She deserved it. Why should I have self-control when she never did? Who was going to believe her anyway? I was the dutiful daughter who came to take care of her. We were friends. She had dementia.

I should be ashamed to say how I pondered the idea for over a minute. Revenge was a foreign idea, and I needed to understand what part of my psyche it was coming from. I made the sound and moral decision not to hurt her in any way. Yet there was a part of me, a piece of my inner child, who couldn't accept it. So I acted out in other ways; I ate her food.

Mom was a terrible eating addict. That's why she portioned our food. Mom didn't want us to get fat like her. She didn't know I'd find her candy stash after the holidays in her closet. She didn't know I'd find baking ingredients and try to make cakes without recipes. She didn't know I'd sneak into other people's houses to raid their pantry because one packet of instant oatmeal wasn't enough for a growing girl's breakfast.

Now Mom was retired, she kept her Costco-sized licorice, chips, and ice cream in plain sight. My way of revenge was eating her snacks. I had a sense of guilty pleasure knowing she couldn't stop me. I didn't realize it then, but it was my replacement for hurting her.

Over that time, Mom thanked me for the help. She made it known she appreciated us moving to take care of her. Yet there was no great catharsis. Then one afternoon, after a day of appointments and pharmacies, Mom crawled into bed at 5 pm.

"You are sacrificing your life for me," she said, like an explorer discovering something.

I didn't know what to say. I mumbled something about not worrying about it. I wanted to say: "As a mother should do for her child.". Again, I chose the high road of silence.

We threw a surprise 80th birthday party. The last one Mom had. She loved the attention, and it marked the beginning of her final decline. Every week there were more symptoms, less remembering, and less desire to do anything but watch TV, eat, and sleep.

The last month was the hardest. Mom became unpredictable, and I had to put more and more safeguards around her autonomy. She would take several days of medicine at one time. Sometimes she'd search the cabinets for a pill she thought she was missing. I kept dialing back the things she was in charge of. Then it was becoming difficult for her to walk. I watched the woman who dominated my life become helpless and frail.

The doctor told me we could get assistance if we signed up for hospice. I needed someone to make her shower. She needed a hospital bed and a wheelchair. The intake nurse spent over an hour with us, and Mom was barely awake to contribute. The nurse told me to expect a gradual decline over several months. However, hospice only lasted ten days.

Every day something new happened. I started sleeping at Mom's house because she fell when she got out of bed. She manipulated every bed barrier we bought and refused to call out for me at night. Usually, I could hear her stirring and hustled to help her into the bathroom. Until the night I woke up to a thud. It was so loud it shook the house.

Mom was flat on her back, a pool of blood oozing into the carpet. She was conscious but not mentally present for the paramedics.

Nor did she remember getting ten staples in her head at the hospital, and she tried to pick at them.

Several days later, she couldn't walk. Then she didn't have the strength to get in and out of the wheelchair. Then the worst indignity possible for my mother; she couldn't go to the toilet even with my assistance.

She insisted on a catheter and held her bladder for over an hour while we waited for the hospice nurse to come. She cried in pain, and I rubbed her feet to distract her. She didn't realize she would have to wear adult diapers anyway.

After the catheter was in place, Mom looked at the ceiling.

"What are you looking at, Rose?" the gentle hospice nurse asked.

"Jesus," Mom said.

"What is he doing?"

Mom was silent.

"Is he just looking at you?" the nurse asked, and Mom nodded.

It was odd because Mom was not religious. That was my department.

The next day Mom was sleepy and restless. She tried to climb the wall on the side of her bed. When the nurses came out to show me how to change her adult diaper, I knew I had reached my limit. I could not change this woman's diapers. I put a call out to everyone I knew to find a nurse or home help. That was around noon.

At 1 pm, Mom became lucid. She had me repeat, for the millionth time, what was happening to her, but somehow she understood this time.

"Your heart is worn out, Mom. There's nothing more we can do."

"Can I get a heart transplant?"

I tried not to choke up.

"No, Mom, they won't give hearts to people over 80."

"Are there other medicines we can try?"

"No. We've tried all the medicines."

"Am I dying?"

"Mom, you've always been a straight shooter, so I'll be straight with you. Yes, this is it. But it's going to be ok. I'm keeping you home like you always wanted. I won't let them take you to the hospital. The nurse brought some medicine in case you are in pain. I'm going to stay with you the whole time."

"Ok," she said, and that was it.

By 4 pm, I called the nurse for dosages of the pain meds. Mom became violently restless, yet asleep. I was afraid she was going to hurt herself. Every hour I was on the phone with the nurse until 9 pm. I dripped meds onto Mom's tongue as instructed. The effects barely lasted an hour.

My husband and I sat with Mom all evening. We put on soothing music and prayed the prayers for the dying. I held her hand and told her it was ok. I told her I'd take care of her animals, and everything would be alright. By 10 pm, I was exhausted and went to lie down until the next dose of medicine. At 11 pm, Mom was gone.

It took an hour for the hospice nurse to come. It was another hour after that for the funerary men to find us. In those hours, I was in shock, relieved, and carried a hefty portion of anger.

I didn't have a mother to mourn. I mourned something greater: all that could have been. The past months she showed me a woman I'd never known. She told me things I never knew and broke my heart every day.

I thought of all the ways my life would have been different. I thought of how my children could have had a relationship with their grandma rather than a periodic obligatory visit. My mother robbed all of us and herself of the fullness of life. Our family could have been united, supportive, and loving.

Before they zipped up the black bag, I had to ask one more time.

"Are we sure she's dead? I just want to make sure. There would be nothing worse than waking up in a bag."

"Yes. I'm sure." the nurse said. "There is nothing more you can do. She is gone."

My daughter was on a plane the next day. She didn't care to see her grandmother off but wanted to support me. She came because I dissolved the family curse. I hope that's what I've done.

I never let my children feel unloved, unwanted, and alone. When my children send me in a body bag, I hope there won't be regrets. Hopefully, they will know they were loved and never yearn for what could have been.

Hopefully, my mom is looking down, proud I did that.

BROOKE O'CONNOR

"More and more women are realizing that only collective
strength and action will allow us to be free to fight for the kind of
society that meets basic human needs."

Roxanne Dunbar

8

———————————

MY DUMP BOX
THE TOOL I USE TO SURVIVE

"If you are always trying to be normal, you will never know how amazing you can be." Maya Angelou

I had finally settled into my new home, new job, and new life. I was organizing my bedroom closet, pulling everything out, and putting shelves up. I decided I would go through the boxes that were in there and throw out or give away anything I no longer need. I have been dragging so much with me from home to home.

Carrying memories, I couldn't let go of the past. I came across a heavy box. I knew what was in there, I always just brush this one aside. I don't remember a lot about the content, but it is a box that has a name, it is my Dump box.

I know you want to know what a dump box is. Well, it is a box that has all my dump books and a few other things. So, I'm sure you want to know what a dump book is. A dump book is like a journal, it is a book that is kept at my bedside, and I dump all the shit that I can't always forget about. It is the stuff that wakes you up in the middle of the night, the shit that seeps into your head and you just can't forget about it. It's the trauma and the stresses of all the tragedies that life has brought. This is the tool that I use to survive!!

A little back story on what brought me to the point that I needed to make myself a dump book. I grew up in a home with my two younger brothers, my mom, and my stepdad.

My mom came from an abusive background herself. Her mother and father were both alcoholics. Her father passed away when she was 14. She very shortly after left her family home to run away to New Brunswick with my father. A much older man. He was 39. She eventually got pregnant with me at the age of 17. Then only 14 months later she had my brother Vic, and Bobby followed three years later.

My father was a very violent and abusive man. She fled New Brunswick with the three of us in hopes of a better life for herself and her children. My mom did try, but I think it was hard for her. She told me often "I did the best with what I had." I am sure that in her mind she believed that.

She hadn't had the best examples set for her in life. My mother didn't drink or do drugs, and for that I am grateful. I think, in some way, she was almost afraid to drink because of what she had seen as a child. However, my mom became very abusive towards my brothers and me. I think she thought if she hit us, we would behave, but that didn't work. It made us act out more at times. There wasn't a lot of affection in our home from our mom. I remember trying to snuggle with her and her asking "What do you want?"

I do remember a time when my mom was fun. I remember her laughing and dancing. I think a time came somewhere around the age of nine. My mom had just bought her first home. I remember her always worrying about what the neighbors would think.

I think owning a home and three young kids at the age of 26 was a lot of stress for her. Back then, kids were meant to be seen and not heard. We were kids who missed our dad, who didn't live in the same province, and we weren't allowed to speak to him. This brought a lot of emotions for us. When we spoke of him, we were told he didn't want us. This hurt, and we would act out.

I remember, one time, food went missing. My mom and stepdad asked who took it. No one would admit to it, so my parents lined us in the living room and my dad took his belt and proceeded to spank each of us on the bum with it until someone admitted to taking the food. Eventually, one of my brothers admitted to taking it because we didn't want to get hit anymore. The more they hit, the harder they would hit.

This was the beginning of the continuous beatings to get us to be better children. As we got older, the beatings got worse. They would use whatever they could grab and hit us wherever they could hit. Of course, we became squirmy. We would try to avoid getting hit. This only made it worse. We would get hit on the head, the face, the back. It really didn't matter. We were told it was our fault because we moved too much.

When I was nine, my stepdad molested me. He would sneak into my room at night while my mom was at work and touch me. I remember being so scared to tell anyone. I told my best friend, and she told her mom. She spoke to me and told me I had to tell my mom. She said if I didn't tell my mom, she would.

Finally, one night I lay in my mom's bed and told her about it. She phoned my stepdad and had him come over and talk. The next day she told me that he said he didn't touch me, and I must be confused. She told me that he was looking at my tummy, that the doctor said I had worms, and if you shine a flashlight on my tummy, you could see them. I told my mom that I knew that wasn't what happened, and she told me there was no way he could have touched me. He is a good man and would never do that.

From then on, I knew that no one would ever believe me. He never touched me again, but I still had to live with the fact that my mom didn't believe me. I was told never to speak of this again.

At the age of 14, I was sent to live with my father in Montreal. My father loved me very much and was great at showing it. My father also came from a very dysfunctional home.

At the age of 14, he lied about his age and joined the army. He saw a lot of very messed up stuff while he was there. This messed with his head in a terrible way. My father one night crawled into bed with me and tried to touch me inappropriately. I jumped out of my bed and told him to stop. He got up and told me he was sorry, and we never spoke of it again. I was eventually sent back to live in BC with my mom and stepdad. I heard my mom one day telling her friend about what had happened to me. She told her friend that she knew that was going to happen to me. When her friend asked why she sent me there, she replied, "She needed to learn it for herself."

I became a very promiscuous girl at a young age, curious about sex. I had boyfriends very young, when I was 15, I met a guy who I thought I was in love with. At the age of 16, I ran away from home to live with him. My mom found me and took me back home. I told her that I didn't want to live at home anymore and that he and I had a plan to save money and move out. My mom told me that I wasn't going to wait until I could save up. She told me I had to pack my stuff and leave now. She took me to my aunts and dropped me off. She told me I couldn't come back home.

My two younger brothers were sent away as well. One of those brothers went to live in a group home and the other one in the Maple's treatment center.

I couldn't stay with my aunt for very long because she had three other children that she couldn't afford to support. I ended up living with my nan for a while I got myself a job at McDonald's and then moved in with a lady named Pearl.

I babysat Pearl's son at night while she went to school to become a radio announcer. I didn't stay there for very long I can't really remember why I had to move, but I moved in with my boyfriend again.

That didn't last long. He was very heavy-handed, and before long, he kicked me out. I went and stayed with a girlfriend named Deedee for a while until I found my own place. By this time, I realized I was pregnant. Seventeen years old, on my own, and going to have a baby. When I told my boyfriend that I was pregnant, he told me he wanted nothing to do with the baby or me.

I lived on my own until I was about seven months pregnant, then he decided that he was going to move in with me. I thought that was going to be great; I was going to have a baby, and the baby's dad and I would live together and be happy. That wasn't the case, I had two more children, and I spent six years on and off in a very abusive relationship.

At the age of 21, I knew I had to get out of that home. I knew I had to give my kids a better life. My oldest daughter had sat on the bathroom counter and watched her father beat me severely in front of her like it was nothing. Again, another home of physical violence and mental abuse that I needed to leave. I was 21 single mom of three children ages 2 ½, 1 ½, and three months.

Shortly after, I met another man. I truly fell in love with him and had two children with him. We thought life couldn't get better. Unfortunately, when you're a kid having kids, and you haven't had the best examples set for you, you don't really know how to be a grown-up and raise children properly.

We fought a lot. Times were tough, and money was really tight. He had a really hard time holding a job down. I loved him very much, but because of the past traumas I had, I didn't know how to show love to anyone other than my children. Eventually, he and I split up, and I became a single mom with five children.

We had talked of getting back together, but he had gone down the wrong path by this point. He started to get involved with drugs and criminal activity, and it was something that I couldn't have our children around. A few years later, he went missing, presumed drowned.

When I got the phone call from his mother, I dropped to the floor to my knees. I started crying. I'd never felt so sick in my life. I thought I was going to throw up. There was a pain that I'd never felt. I had only just spoken to him a few days prior.

I had a hard time believing that it was true and had never really been able to come to terms with his loss. I didn't know how to cope with the loss of him and the unknown of whether he was alive or dead.

I ended up in therapy trying to learn how to cope with being a single mom telling my kids that their dad had drowned and trying to raise them the best I could. This is where I learned about the importance of taking everything out of your brain and putting it somewhere else. This is where I learned how to write my dump book.

I was just a child, 18 years old, when I had my first. I grew up with my children, and for that, I am so grateful. We taught each other how to have fun. I know I made mistakes along the way, but we all do. For me, the most important thing was for my children to know they were loved.

I went through a lot in my life, and I have had a lot of people ask me if I could change anything in my life, what would it be? Everything in my life brought me to be the person I am today, and it has helped Me Too! So definitely not! So many men and women, children, and teenagers become survivors themselves. My answer? Absolutely nothing!

A lot of things that I went through that were extremely hard, and at times I could never understand the reason behind being beaten or being molested and so many other things that I have endured. I believe that everything I have gone through has given me the ability to help others work through their trauma. I have had a lot of people whom I have given words of survival, words to hold hope. They have said my experience has helped them to survive, so every single thing that I have experienced in my life has brought me to where I am today. When I look at it in that way, it really makes it all worth it.

I have often tried to understand why I chose men who were abusive. By using the tool of my dump book, I have learned that my definition of love was abuse.

The one person in this world who is supposed to love you unconditionally is your parents. Your mom, the woman who carried you and gave you life. My first husband would continuously tell me can't you see how much I love you? My mother always told me that she wanted what was best for us that is why we got the beatings that we got.

I had to learn to move past all the abuse. I was always told I had to learn to forgive. I felt I just needed to learn to move past all of the abuse and to learn to forgive myself for accepting it. I am in a far better place in my life where I've learned how well I can take care of myself.

I have spent a very large part of my life in survival mode. A survivor of mental, physical, and sexual abuse. That, too, is not the best way to live.

Today my children are grown, and I have become an independent, self-sufficient woman. I own a small business and am successful in my job.

Writing this book has brought out some other emotions. It's made me realize how difficult it is for me to speak about myself. I still struggle with complimenting myself. Even though I have learned to accept compliments openly and learned to be proud of myself for my successes, I still have a hard time speaking about my successes. Again the inner voice tells me that I'm not good enough. It's not surprising. It's what I heard all my life.

I have been on my own, commitment-free, for the last two years. The kids have grown up and moved on. During these last two years, I have been trying to learn to love and accept myself. A part of that is learning to trust myself. It is a slow process of trusting my decisions in my life and not relying on others to tell me what I should do.

I have made a huge career change and am continuing to educate myself for further career advancement. I have learned that I can love my mom and still not be involved in the turmoil that comes along with having her in my life. At the time of writing this book, it has been 14 years since I spoke to my mom and my stepdad.

I have learned that I need to make small promises to myself and keep them in order to rebuild my trust in myself. I am teaching myself to love ME unconditionally. This is a chain that needs to be broken in my family more than any other chain. By doing this, it will break all the others.

See, I loved my children unconditionally but forgot about the most important person, myself.

You can't be the best mom/ wife/ friend if you don't love and respect yourself. You will always attract abusers in one way or another if you don't start with you. Love yourself the way you want others to love you.

Don't allow anyone to treat you disrespectfully. By stopping the abuse, I have been respecting myself. Doing this for myself will allow me to break the chain of abusive relationships and teach my sons, daughters, and grandchildren that we deserve the very best. I hope this is how my children will learn too.

My wish is that my grandchildren and great-grandchildren will continue to break the chains in our family history.

LORETTA LEBRETON

"I do not try to dance better than anyone else. I only try to dance better than myself."

Arianna Huffington

9

BEYOND THE PAIN
LIVING WITH FIBROMYALGIA

"Pain is a microphone, and it does me no good unless I transform it into something that is." Lady Gaga

One day I awoke to permanent headaches that just never seemed to stop. When I finally counted, they were lasting between 20 and 25 days a month. I could not figure out what was happening to me and why they felt so intense, often sending me on a journey of exploration of the sublime atonement of this never-ending pain I had been experiencing and the symptoms that emerged and seemed connected in some way.

From numbness in my hands to ongoing neck pain and inflammation, vomiting, peeing my pants because I was vomiting so hard, and days in bed, to name a few. I have always had migraines, even as a kid, but these ongoing ones were the worst. They affected my job and my activities of daily life and would have me isolated as a result.

My social circle soon became the emergency department, my family doctor, and several other doctors, as we tried to get to the root of what I was experiencing. Never did the medical professionals question me as being "crazy" or say that "it was all in my mind" and other limiting beliefs that would have made me doubt myself.

Instead, they would rub my back, hold the vomit bag, and would often question whether it was meningitis, in fact. As they took such good care of me, I wish that after those visits, some of them could have taken me home and continued the care. It was amazing, and it felt so good to feel cared for after living alone for such a long time.

At work, I was often vomiting in off-the-road places and in so much pain that I started to miss days of work. Working as a Continuing Care Assistant, I felt it wasn't fair to my clients to have someone showing up who was not able to care for them as they deserved. They would often say, "You don't look well, are you okay? Lie down on my bed if you like and have a sleep. I won't tell!" I would say, "No, I am fine, thank you anyways, and I am here for you, not me."

The Nurse Manager at work would often suggest I go on Long Term Disability, which would make me very upset and doubt my abilities in fighting whatever this was I was experiencing. They felt that if I got injured, it may be more detrimental to my health moving forward. Looking back, I think they really did have my best interest at heart.

When I first got my letter from the employer concerning my missed days at work, I immediately contacted the person responsible for this new policy. It motivated me to become proactive in my recovery. This Wellness Consultant for the

Health Authority ended up being my biggest supporter and helped me a lot on the job. She worked with me for about 2-3 years before everyone decided that I needed to take those two years off to sort out these ongoing health concerns I was having.

Of course, it was the union that solidified the icing on this enormous situation concerning my life, my future, and my career. I had worked as a Continuing Care Assistant for almost 24 years at that time and had tried many times to get a job change but was often rejected, thinking I had to be there the rest of my life. I would get criticized for not wanting to take care of Seniors, told that it was a good job, and so forth.

I questioned all of those comments coming from people who were making it more about them than me, as I may have been developing some compassion fatigue as well at that time. It was a rewarding career where you saw a lot, and the responsibilities were huge, especially in home and community care. Often dealing with family members living in the home, caregivers who were getting fatigued as well, and often dumping their ongoing emotional and physical ailments when they had the chance to. There were other workers who would do things not required or on.

The care plans the clinician implemented were for everyone's safety and concern. This would create unnecessary conflict between workers and patients, a triad, a coup, and if you didn't do what they wanted and those care aides did, you were punished in some way which is how it felt at that time.

I saw that those workers were compassionate and cared deeply about their patient's welfare, but for some reason, the clinician saw a bigger picture and why those directions were in place in the patient's homes and wished as well that those workers would stop. There were unexpected home deaths where you were the last person, along with their spouse, to experience their loved one's last breath. Not being trained in any of that, you often had to hold in your emotions as you wanted to remain professional and present, so you would stuff your own feelings in support of theirs.

As all these memories, frustrations, aches, and pains flooded me, I saw my life changing and not within my control. I fell apart. I started with six months of therapy which really helped my mental health, which is also recognized and called PTSD.

I always thought PTSD was for the military and what the military after World War Two called "shell shock," never thinking that PTSD could also be vicarious trauma that included burnout and compassion fatigue.

As I followed up with my family doctor regarding the counselor's thoughts, we soon agreed on generalized anxiety and adjustment disorder. That diagnosis made more sense, even though my anxiety and panic attacks would be triggered by people who made me feel threatened and brought to mind the bullying I had faced a few years prior.

Perhaps that incident was the one that changed my life forever, causing ongoing physical, emotional, and mental pain. I have written about my situation involving an RV Park I was living in and the circumstances that surrounded it in another chapter I wrote for "Shine Volume 3: Choosing Success Over Adversity". My publisher thought I should write a book about overcoming adversity. However, it has taken me far too long to bounce back from all of this.

I just wasn't feeling like I was resilient as I had been so many times in my past, so how could I honestly write about something I wasn't feeling? I was not just letting it roll past me effortlessly and buoyantly. I was stuck in my pain in those moments that knocked me down and felt like they finished me for good.

I felt like a boxer in a ring, receiving so many punches to my body and face that I feel lifeless on the floor and not receiving any reward after, except the one I would have to dig deep for. What was the lesson, and what had I not prepared myself for so that I could have avoided this altogether? That question we all ask ourselves, "Why Me?" I can't take it anymore.

Well, the pity party didn't last for long, as I proactively stepped out of my comfort zone and accepted what was. We can allow ourselves to stay stuck, or we can choose another approach to how we handle the difficulties we find ourselves in, those ones that make us stop and think. It was in this dark time that I was encouraged. I looked at how I could problem solve and the solutions I might find in my quest for another purpose.

Purpose is that motivating factor that drives you towards something tangible, a feeling of satisfaction for accomplishing that goal or helping someone else. I was asked if I would be interested in taking over the Shoebox Project for Women in Shelters. It was here that I felt compassion like I had not before. This compassion was a sense of understanding how women in shelters and struggling with homelessness must feel because I was one step toward being there.

It cemented that belief I had about anyone who can find themselves in desperate situations, often completely out of their control. Here I found satisfaction in giving a new direction in my life. Those four years were what I needed. I had started this before long-term disability and carried it forward because I knew it needed to be done. My service was of need to the community I resided in. I stepped into an unknown state that introduced me to new circles, people who also cared for this vulnerable population, and a sense of belonging was felt by all who gave, no matter how big or small.

When I was told by my Physiotherapist that he thought I had fibromyalgia, it all started to make sense. The headaches, which the neurologist confirmed, co-existed with fibromyalgia, pain points, extreme tiredness, and more. I took those two years to not only help others but work on understanding myself, what I was able to tolerate, where I needed to stop and take a break, and where my mind just needed to rest.

I took a Kundalini yoga class and learned meditation. These both really helped calm my nervous system, helping me to achieve some success in my physical goals and my mind also. It aided my digestive system as I slowed down enough to enjoy every morsel on my plate, the flavor of what was in my mouth, the texture and how it felt and looked, and most importantly, how it made my body feel and look at the emotions that rose up with each bite.

Today I am much better. I am healthier in my body, mind, and soul. Trusting much more in myself while becoming much more emotional than before. Sensitivity is a part of me and always has been but even more so than before my fall and getting bullied in a park; now I just feel it more in the way of tears, which help me to self-soothe rather than hold all that in.

Emotions are not fixed but genuine, and they no longer impose chronic headaches as they had in the past. I was so afraid to cry because these headaches would last for days. I was not able to just let them go! This is what has become something I have resided at working through, along with the anxiety I no longer feel either. It took a conscious effort and a move away from a state I felt stuck in, away from situations that altered my course in life.

As a result, I have risen, like a phoenix in fire, rising new and not defeated, strong and learning about resiliency in a way I had not experienced before. I believe that if we truly want to change, we can.

It takes conscious awakening, love, and nurturing of self, compassion, kind thoughts, and words.

So, I want to encourage those who may be struggling to take that time to rest and focus on awakening offering nurturing thoughts, love, and compassion from that place within. Listening and noticing along the way, from the way you move your body to the choices of food, the words you long to hear, not taking you away from your truth, but recognizing the beauty you have within, letting your light shine.

TRISH SCOULAR

"Well-behaved women seldom make history."

Laurel Thatcher Ulrich

10

MEET THE AUTHORS

As readers, we often dive into the world created by the words on the pages without considering the people behind them. But as we know, authors are the heart and soul of the literary world. They are the ones who craft their stories from their hearts and minds. Sharing their personal stories with us so we can learn from them and possibly gain clarity in our lives.

Sharing stories can be extremely powerful and beneficial. By telling others about our own experiences, you can connect with people who have been through something similar, and you might even inspire them to share their personal stories.

Authors who decide to share their stories are brave and powerful. They know there are people who are willing to listen and support them.

By reading a little bit about an author, the reader can get to know them.

Some authors included their personal contact information should you want to contact them directly or with their business.

Female power, ladies! If YOU or someone YOU know would benefit from knowing any of these lady business owners, don't be bashful! Reach out to them! Let's support one another.

ANNE CAISSIE

Who's That Beautiful Woman In The Mirror?

Finally Finding My Way To A Life Of Body Kindness and Love After 40 Years

Anne Caissie is a women's personal coach who is passionate about empowering women to live their best lives.

With over a decade of experience in the field, Anne has helped countless women overcome their struggles with body image and develop a positive relationship with food and exercise.

Anne offers a range of courses to cater to different needs, including the following:

- 1:1 coaching sessions for personalized guidance.
- The Ditch the Diet Academy is for those looking to break free from restrictive diets and learn intuitive eating.
- Body Kindness Workshops for group support and community building.

With Anne's compassionate and non-judgmental approach, you can expect to feel supported and encouraged every step of the way on your journey toward a happier, healthier you.

If you would like to connect with Anne, you can find her at one of the links below.

https://annecaissie.com/

https://www.facebook.com/groups/thebodykindnesssisterhood

https://www.instagram.com/thebodykindness_sisterhood/

DitchtheDietAcademy@gmail.com

BRENDA COOPER

From City Slicker to Country Picker

Brenda's life is a story of resilience and determination. Although she has experienced many exciting adventures and colorful life, she has overcome unexpected challenges, her journey has not been without hardship and abuse. Despite these challenges, Brenda's strength and willpower have played an instrumental role in shaping her into the woman she is today.

Brenda worked various jobs for several years and was determined to gain experience and broaden her perspectives. Her interest in technology and computers eventually landed her a position at a large trucking company, where she helped implement the company's warehouse operations with a customized inventory management system, however after many years the flame dwindled, and eventually, she left.

Taking a year off and still not wanting to retire she looked for other work which led her down a completely new path, and she soon found herself driving a school bus for special needs children. The job quickly became a passion for her, and she formed close bonds with the children she drove daily, finding it one of her life's most fulfilling jobs.

Brenda's passion for writing has been a lifelong fascination, and after retiring, she eagerly returned to her pen. Her work has since been published four times in Women Like Me Community Books, and twice in Women Like Me. She is currently working on a book of her own, which she hopes to publish soon.

Brenda's writing is deeply personal and draws from her own experiences of navigating through some of life's most challenging moments. Despite the difficult memories, she writes from the heart and has found the process to be tremendously therapeutic. Brenda is incredibly grateful for the unwavering support of her loving husband, with whom she has shared 25 wonderful years, and her beautiful children, who constantly encourage her to pursue her passion for writing.

The adventures were far from over. Brenda and her husband shared a dream of owning a small piece of land in the countryside, and they made that dream come true by purchasing their own hobby farm. Now, Brenda's days begin early, tending to their beloved animals, including a flock of sheep, seasonal pigs, chickens, and six dogs. In the afternoons, she, and her husband work on various projects, from building new dwellings for their animals to expanding paddocks.

Despite the hard work, Brenda and her husband find immense joy and fulfillment in their hobby farm and love sharing the experience with their friends and family. For Brenda, it's not just a pastime, but a way of life that brings her closer to nature, self-sufficiency, and a sense of purpose that she has always been searching for. Her story is a testament to the power of determination and following one's dreams.

TRACY DIONNE

Finding Gratefulness in Grief

The Journey of a Deep-seeded Friendship through Love and Loss Transformed into Daily Gratitude

Tracy is an elementary school teacher and a proud mother of two boys. She enjoys her family life with her husband of over 12 years.

She attended Kwantlen University and then moved to the University of the Fraser Valley to complete her Bachelor of Arts Degree with a minor in psychology. She then moved to Prince George, British Columbia, for two years to obtain her Bachelor of Education Degree.

Tracy enjoys staying active by running. She also loves the beach and traveling to new places. She has a bucket list of places she wants to visit over the years.

She recently attended a paint and sip night and now enjoys painting with acrylic paints in her free time. Tracy loves to explore nature and spend time on the water in the summer boating, kayaking, and paddle boarding.

If you would like to reach out to Tracy, you can contact her by email:

Tracydionne77@gmail.com or macdonald914@hotmail.com

SHERON CHISHOLM

Little Girl Looking to Be Loved

Finding the Love Changed Her Life

Sheron was born in Guelph, Ontario, Canada, and at the age of five, her family moved to Pontiac, Michigan, where she grew up.

She decided early in life that she wanted to be a nurse, and so she did. Sheron attended Oakland Community College and Wayne State University, ending with a Master of Science in Nursing.

She practiced in several settings, but her favorite was in-home care and home hospice. She was involved in the early growth of hospice in Michigan, was on the governor's committee to write the rules and regulations for hospice, and was the manager of the first hospice programs in Michigan to be licensed and certified.

Sheron held administrative positions in-home care for most of her career and continued to provide services directly to patients, which is her passion. She enjoyed working directly with patients and their families to see them embrace the changes their illness required so that they could meet their life goals. Working with patients and their families was a twenty-four-hour professional, including serving as a leader and consultant for staff caring for patients.

Early in her career, she was active in professional organizations and assisted in the growth of nursing as a profession in Michigan Nurses Association and Hospice Organization. Apart from her career, she loves to travel both on personal trips and mission trips with her church to Haiti and Lithuania. She has sponsored six children through Compassion International and has had the privilege of visiting two of them in Kenya and Bolivia.

One of her passions was being a Girl Scout all the way through to Senior High and then being a leader when she lived in Petoskey, MI.

She finally was a Leader for her daughter's troop in Traverse City. Yes, she had children!

After she had accomplished most of her career goals and was still not married, she decided since she always had a passion for children, she would adopt. Sheron adopted three children from the same family but at different times, two girls and one boy. Their ages at the time of adoption were 13, 6, and 9.

The children are now grown and married, and she has one grandson. The later part of my career was focused on giving the children all the cultural, social, and educational experiences possible. They played instruments and were involved in sports, including gymnastics, horseback riding, and scouts. Sheron enjoyed them as much as the children, and most of all. She enjoyed traveling with them to Chicago, New York, Canada, where her extended family still lived, and Toronto, to name a few.

Now somewhat retired, Sheron's passion is to work with women who have chronic pain and teach alternative natural methods to achieve pain management. She coached hundreds of patients to achieve management of pain and is beginning her entrepreneur business to continue her work in retirement.

If you would like to contact Sheron, she is available at:

sheronchisholm@gmail.com

You can also reach her on social media at:

https://Facebook.com/vitalityseekerswithsheron

ROXANNE NAISTUS

Losing My First Love

Healing Through the Guilt and Trauma of Suicide

My name is Roxanne Naistus, and I am from Onion Lake First Nation, Saskatchewan, Canada.

I am 49 years old, a Mother of four, and a Grandmother of 6. I currently run my own home business, Readings By Roxy, out of Lloydminster, Saskatchewan. I offer a number of different services as a Certified Reiki Energy Healer, Certified Massage Therapist, and Certified Angel Card Reader for the past ten years.

Being a First Nations women, we were taught just to take what has happened and don't complain. I just couldn't do that. I have had to stand up for myself and my children more than once in this life!

The reason I chose to share my story here was two things.

After speaking with Julie, the Founder of Women Like Me, I knew this was a safe space where I could be real and open.

Next is that I know there are so many other women going through what I have gone through in my life.

I was so incredibly thankful to be a part of something so positive for creating awareness for Women. One thing I have learned through my own healing journey is that when women unite, the universe turns that energy into something amazing.

Ask, Believe, Receive!

I look forward to connecting with more Warrior Women like me.

If you would like to connect with Roxanne, you can find her here…

https://www.facebook.com/RoxyNaistus?mibextid=ZbWKwL

LETICIA RODRIGUEZ

Trauma Bond

Recovering From Abuse and Healing Through Shadow Work

Leticia was born and raised in Toronto, Ontario, but currently resides in Alberta. A long-time fitness trainer and nutritionist, Leticia's dream came true when she earned her IFBB Elite Pro Card as a competitive bodybuilder in the Figure/Bodyfitness category in 2019.

Her passions include weightlifting, yoga, camping, snorkeling, animals, writing, and photography. When she's not working, you can find her at the gym training for her next competition, relaxing with friends, or hiking in nature with her adorable American Bulldog, Ghost.

Becoming a published author in the Women Like Me series has been a blessing for Leticia. Writing is something that's always come naturally to her, having graduated from school in Ontario with honors and being awarded the Ontario Scholar designation for her high achievements in English and Creative Writing.

Bouncing between multiple areas of interest – from Geology to attaining a diploma in Graphic Design -- Leticia discovered her love of fitness in her late twenties. She was published in Oxygen Women's Fitness Magazine in 2007 after her second competition.

Now in her mid-forties, she plans to expand upon her expertise in physical fitness by venturing into the fields of life and spiritual coaching. Leticia intensely believes that optimal wellness includes physical, mental, emotional, and spiritual components.

She is currently pursuing additional certifications in sports nutrition, reiki, and counseling and recently became trained in numerology.

Leticia hopes that her ongoing story of going within to heal from abuse, toxic relationships, and depression will help other young adults who may be experiencing similar struggles.

Creating and publishing her own books and self-improvement courses are high on her list of future goals!

Leticia's favorite phrase to live by is:

"You are always one decision away from a completely different life." – Mel Robbins.

@letty_ifbbelitepro

@_elev8ted_wellness_

letty.ifbbelitepro@gmail.com

· · ·

BROOKE O'CONNOR

The Golden Years

Forgiveness Isn't Pretty

Brooke is a proud mother, wife, and world traveler. She is currently enjoying life on the Oaxaca, Mexico coast and writing her memoir.

She spent 20+ years in the coaching industry and is now helping other coaches develop their businesses with a blend of authenticity and technology.

If you'd like to talk with Brooke about speaking engagements, coach development, or tacos, you can find her on Facebook:

https://www.facebook.com/brookeoconnor555/

LORETTA LEBRETON

My Dump Box

The Tool I Use to Survive

Loretta was born in New Brunswick. At the age of five, her mother fled with her and her two younger brothers, aged four and one year old, to Vancouver, British Columbia.

Her mother was leaving an abusive relationship in hopes of providing a better life for her three children. Loretta spent her youth growing up in Vancouver, BC.

Loretta is a single mom of five grown children, three girls and two boys. She also has a grandson and a granddaughter, with one more sweet baby girl on the way.

Today Loretta resides in Abbotsford, BC, and works in the film industry. The hours are long, but she enjoys the job. She has a wonderful work family and is so fortunate to be able to meet many interesting people. There is something new every day.

Loretta is currently working towards getting her class 1 driver's license. This will enable her to do more within the industry.

Loretta's passion is creating lovely Memory Bears from loved ones' clothing after they have passed. She has been doing this since 2015 and has made close to 1000 bears. These were sad times and Loretta was glad to have brought some comfort to the families that she has made these for.

She also makes Christmas stockings during the Holiday season and many other items.

Loretta is writing this chapter in hopes to help others who may have gone through similar times. She believes you have a choice, you can be a victim of your story, or you can be the survivor in it. Loretta's choice is always to be a survivor and to help other people find strength within.

She wants you to know that you are not alone.

You can find Loretta on social media…

Visit LeBreton's Nest on Facebook

https://www.facebook.com/profile.php?id=100076304825288&mibextid=ZbWKwL

Instagram - Loretta LeBreton

https://www.instagram.com/lorettaalebreton/

TRISH SCOULAR

Beyond The Pain

Living With Fibromyalgia

Trish is a Wellness Advocate, Registered Professional Counsellor, and Best Selling Author and has been helping others most of her life.

Empathy and listening have always been skills that have come naturally to her since she was a child. Trish would actively listen to those she interacted with, including friends and family, gathering necessary details that helped her develop meaningful relationships throughout her life. She has often been called a Highly Sensitive Person.

Trish has been a Registered Professional Counselor since 2011, following a career as a Long Term Care Aide for 26 years, where she was thoughtful in meeting the needs of her client's overall mental and physical health. It was important for her to take the time to meet the needs of clients coming from a place of compassion, empathy, kindness, and care.

The past 26 years of working in Health Care made Trish realize that she needed more education. That is why she advanced in Applied Psychology and Counselling, which helped create positive interactions between herself, the families, and the other nursing supports that were in place.

Trish became a strong advocate for those who needed an added voice, working together with family and other team members that supported their emotional, mental, physical, and spiritual needs were met, allowing them to improve their quality of life.

Trish was a Continuing Care Assistant to clients who were high risk in psychiatry, palliative care, and Dementia/Alzheimer's, had mobility issues, and worked in home care, acute care, emergency care, critical care, and transporting stable patients by ambulance. She supported the client's activities of daily living, giving medications and other details that were necessary in meeting the client's goals from a detailed care plan.

Trish is also an Artist, Kundalini 100 Hour Yoga Instructor, Mindfulness Practitioner, Reiki Master/Teacher, and Clinical Counsellor.

If you would like to reach out to Trish, you can do that here…

Amazon Author Profile

https://www.amazon.com/stores/author/B09S6125R2/about

Facebook

https://www.facebook.com/guidingheartsest?mibextid=LQQJ4d

Trish's Website

https://guiding-hearts.com/

"Owning our story can be hard but not nearly as difficult as spending our lives running from it."

Brené Brown

"If you can't go straight ahead, you go around the corner."

Cher

PART 2

ABOUT WOMEN LIKE ME

11

MEET THE FOUNDER OF WOMEN LIKE ME

Okay, ladies, listen up! This lady is the real deal. She's an author, an entrepreneur, and the founder of a super cool book program, Women Like Me, that was created to empower and inspire you! She has a total of 21 books, and some of these topics include sales tactics and business development.

As an expert in the field of marketing and sales, Julie has provided strategic advice to many well-known companies. She has spoken at a variety of organizations and businesses, where she shares her expertise with entrepreneurs.

Girl, let me tell you about Julie! She has always been passionate about helping other women achieve their dreams, so she started a program to help ladies write their stories in books. She helps these women become published authors and get them the recognition they deserve.

In addition to working with her company, Women Like Me, Julie is also a mentor and coach, assisting women in improving their skills and confidence to succeed at work and in other aspects of their lives. She is passionate about uplifting females and encouraging them to achieve their objectives. Her efforts have benefited hundreds of women.

"I want to build a community where women of all races can communicate and ... continue to support and take care of each other. I want to give women a space to feel their own strength and tell their stories. That is power."

Beyonce

12

JULIE FAIRHURST

Julie Fairhurst is the Founder of the Women Like Me Book Program. She is also a Certified Master Persuader, Sales Strategies, and Storyteller Coach. She started the Women Like Me Project to help women tell their stories. She helps her clients to share their message with the world through her unique storytelling programs. To her credit, Julie has published 21 books and has over a hundred published authors.

Sales and marketing expert Julie helps women entrepreneurs build their influence and authority with their clients and customers, so they can increase their revenue and profits. With a certification in persuasion, as well as over 30 years of sales and marketing experience, Julie is an expert at understanding human behavior and what triggers people to make a purchase. She helps her clients to develop marketing strategies that appeal to their target audience, and she also provides coaching on how to close the sale.

In addition, she teaches her clients how to use the power of storytelling to engage and connect with their customers. As a result, they are able to build trust and credibility, which leads to more sales and higher conversion rates.

Julie is also a sought-after speaker, trainer, and prevention educator. She has been delivering empowering workshops to adolescents and adults on the issues affecting their safety. She has presented to organizations such as the Vancouver Police Department, Justice Institute, University of British Columbia, and Capilano College. Behavioral Society of British Columbia, Surrey Memorial Hospital. Teachers Association of North Vancouver, and Shine Live, as well as appearing on television and in video.

When Julie was young, her home life was chaotic and tumultuous. Her parents were constantly fighting, and she felt unsafe and unloved. As a result, she developed some bad habits and made some poor decisions. As a teenager, she was headed down the wrong path, and it seemed like there was no hope for her.

But, somewhere deep inside, that little girl inside of her showed up and reminded her that she wanted better for herself and for her kids. Julie had no support from anyone, not a soul. She had to do it all on her own. She had no help from anyone, not a single person. She had to do everything by herself.

It's not easy to change your life. In fact, it can be downright difficult. But it's also necessary if you want to move forward. Sometimes, you have to take a step backwards before you can go forward. And that's what happened to Julie.

Julie is a woman who has achieved great success in her life, despite facing many obstacles. She is a great example of someone who did not let anything stand in her way. Despite these challenges, she never gave up. She went back to school and finished her education. She built an outstanding career in sales, marketing, and promotion. She won the company's top awards and was the first woman to achieve top salesperson year after year in a male-dominated industry. She was a sales manager for some of the country's most prestigious developers. She is an inspiration to everyone who knows her. She is proof that anything is possible with hard work and dedication.

Many people say that you should never look back, but Julie does. Why? Because she wants to remember the journey that brought her to where she is today. And today her life is very different.

Then, in 2019, Julie's beautiful 24-year-old niece died from a drug overdose on the streets of Vancouver, Canada. And that was the day she said enough! Her niece's death indirectly resulted from the generational beliefs and abuse that some of her siblings continue with their destructive lifestyles. So, when Julie says, "enough is enough," she means it! Unfortunately, her story isn't unique.

When we don't face our issues, we pass on dysfunctional behaviors to future generations. This is what happened to my young niece. This is why I started the Women Like Me organization. When children grow up in toxic environments, they often develop behavioral issues that follow them into adulthood. This can lead to serious problems in their relationships, career, and mental health. My young niece was a victim of this.

Everyone has a story, and everyone's story matters. No matter what you've been through, you can change your life for the better. It's not always easy, but with determination and perseverance, anything is possible.

The first step is to believe in yourself. You have the power to create whatever future you want for yourself. The next step is to take action. You can't just sit and wait for good things to happen. You have to go out and make them happen. And finally, you have to persevere. There will be setbacks along the way, but that's no reason to give up. Keep going, and never give up on your dreams.

If you're willing to put in the work, you can change your life for the better. You have the power to do so. You just have to believe in yourself and take the steps to make it happen. So don't give up on yourself - you're capable of much more than you think. And when you're ready to get started, I'm here to help.

"A well-read woman is a dangerous creature."

Lisa Kleypas

WANT TO CONNECT WITH JULIE?

Email: julie@changeyourpath.ca

Women Like Me Stories

www.womenlikemestories.com

Find Julie on Social Media:

YouTube – Julie Fairhurst Women Like Me Stores and in Business

https://www.youtube.com/
channel/UChFnLgiUC9mWnvp7jikKBw

Women Like Me on Facebook

https://www.facebook.com/StoryCoachJulieFairhurst

Rock Star Strategies on Facebook

https://www.facebook.com/juliefairhurstcoaching

LinkedIn - Julie Fairhurst Certified Master Persuader

https://www.linkedin.com/in/salesstrategistjuliefairhurst/

Instagram – Women Like Me Stories

https://www.instagram.com/certified_master_persuader/

TikTok – Sales Strategist

https://www.tiktok.com/@juliethesalesstrategist

Facebook – Julie Fairhurst Academy

https://www.facebook.com/julie.fairhurst.7

"I can promise you that women working together – linked, informed, and educated – can bring peace and prosperity to this forsaken planet."

Isabelle Allende

14

A COMMUNITY OF WOMEN LIKE ME

If you do not already belong to the Women Like Me community, I encourage you to consider joining. It is a great place to find support and connect with other women. You can also participate in discussions, ask questions, and share resources.

Joining the WLMC is a great way to connect with women who have similar experiences and to learn from their successes and challenges. It can also be a great way to find mentors and role models. So, if you are a woman looking for support, please consider joining the WLMC. You will not regret it!

The Women Like Me Community is a social network that connects women who share similar interests, goals, and concerns. Whether a working professional or a stay-at-home mom, this community is for you.

The Women Like Me Community - Julie Fairhurst is a Facebook group of like-minded women who want to pay it forward and lift others to promote healing in the world. They believe that by doing this, they can help to create a world that is kinder and more compassionate.

The Women Like Me Community - Julie Fairhurst is a place where you can feel safe and supported. It is a place where you can be yourself and share your story. It is a place where you can find encouragement, inspiration, and connection.

If you have been looking for a community where you can belong, this is it. Don't wait, join today!

Women Like Me Community – Julie Fairhurst

https://www.facebook.com/groups/879482909307802

"I love to see a young girl go out and grab the world by the lapels. Life's a bitch. You've got to go out and kick ass."

Maya Angelou

15

WOMEN LIKE ME BOOK SERIES

Everyone has a story. And oftentimes, those stories can be powerful things that help us learn and grow. But for some people, their stories can be a source of pain. They may feel like they can't escape their past or that their story is holding them back from living their best lives.

If you're one of those people, know that you're not alone. And more importantly, know that there is hope. There are ways to turn your personal story into something positive and to find healing from the past.

One way is to share your story with others. This can be incredibly cathartic, and it can also help others who have been through similar experiences. you process your feelings and work through any trauma you may be carrying around. And finally, don't forget that your story doesn't define you. You are more than your history. You are more than your pain. You are more than your mistakes. You are more than your story. You are strong, you are brave, and you are enough. So don't let your story hold you back.

Writing about your past can be very beneficial, both emotionally and psychologically. You can increase your feelings or well-being and even improve your physical health. When you write about your past experiences, you relive them in your mind. This can help you to process difficult or traumatic events, and it can also provide you with some closure.

Additionally, writing about your past can help you to better understand yourself and work through any unresolved issues. It can also allow you to see yourself in a new light, which can be both healing and empowering. In addition to helping you emotionally, writing about your past can also be beneficial physically. Studies have shown that expressive writing can help to reduce stress, anxiety, and depression. It can also help to improve your immune system function and promote a sense of calm. So, if you're feeling stressed out or overwhelmed, consider picking up a pen and starting to write.

We only have one shot at this life, and it's our only shot. There are no do-overs. There are no second chances. So, we better make the most of it. We only have this one moment right here, right now, and it's the only moment that really matters. We only have so much time on this planet, and we need to spend it wisely. We only have so much energy, and we want to spend it on things that bring us joy. We only have so much love to give, and we want to give it to people who appreciate it.

If you're a woman and you have had life experiences and the world wants to hear from you. Visit my website at www.womelikemestories.com and get in touch. The world will be waiting.

A story is a powerful thing. It can draw you in, take you on a journey, and leave you with a lasting impression. That's why I love listening to other people's stories. Everyone has a story to tell, and I'm always eager to hear a new one.

I want to hear from you. You can reach me by visiting my website and letting me know you're ready to tell your story. The world is waiting to hear what you have to say. So what are you waiting for? Get in touch today!

Women Like Me Stories

https://womenlikemestories.com/tell-your-story/

"We need women at all levels, including the top, to change the dynamic, reshape the conversation, to make sure women's voices are heard and heeded, not overlooked and ignored."

Sheryl Sandberg

16

MORE FROM JULIE FAIRHURST

Julie's books are available on Amazon or the Women Like Me Stories website.

Sales and Personal Growth

Transferring Enthusiasm - The Sales Book For Your Business Growth

Positivity Makes All The Difference

Agent Etiquette – 14 Things You Didn't Learn in Real Estate School

7 Keys to Success – How to Become A Real Estate Badass

30 Days to Real Estate Action – Real Strategies & Real Connections

Why Agents Quit The Business

Women Like Me Book Series

Women Like Me – A Celebration of Courage and Triumphs

Women Like Me – Stories of Resilience and Courage

Women Like Me – A Tribute to the Brave and Wise

Women Like Me – Breaking Through the Silence

Women Like Me – From Loss to Living

Women Like Me – Healing and Acceptance

Women Like Me – Strong Women in Kenya

Women Like Me – Reclaiming Our Power

Women Like Me Community Book Series

Women Like Me Community – Messages to My Younger Self

Women Like Me Community – Sharing Words of Gratitude

Women Like Me Community – Sharing What We Know to Be True

Women Like Me Community – Journal for Self-Discovery

Women Like Me Community – Sharing Life's Important Lessons

Women Like Me Community – Having Better Relationships

Women Like Me Community – Honoring The Women in Our Lives

www.ingramcontent.com/pod-product-compliance
Lightning Source LLC
Chambersburg PA
CBHW051509050726
47594CB00010B/4025